New Mexico Historic Documents

New Mexico Historic Documents

Richard N. Ellis, Editor

UNIVERSITY OF NEW MEXICO PRESS

Albuquerque

Kwa' chuwaya holh yam yakna piya'na tey'amme tun'an
'akka tem taa t'on 'aawona yaa'anna.
(You are responsible for protecting the people;
do not ever fail them.)

—Part of the oath of office for
tribal officers of Zuni Pueblo
(figurative translation)

Contents

Introduction

The key documents of the American past are an essential part of the nation's heritage, but while most Americans are acquainted with the Declaration of Independence or the United States Constitution, they are less familiar with the documents of their state's history. This collection of documents brings together the major documents of New Mexico history from 1821 to the mid twentieth century, although emphasis is on the territorial period. It is but a partial record of New Mexico's past, but it is hoped that a companion volume of documents from the Spanish period will follow.

This is probably the first time that all of the most useful documents on New Mexico history in this period have been gathered into one convenient volume for students and the general public. All documents herein have been available in scattered publications such as compilations of statutes, separate laws and proclamations, editions of the *Blue Book* issued by the secretary of state for New Mexico, and other government publications. In each instance the full, official text, either original or as amended, is given. Any recent translation is so indicated, and all orthography and punctuation is exactly that of the original.

Stephen Watts Kearny's proclamations of July 31 and August 22 were printed in *House Executive Document No. 19,* 29th Congress, 2d session, in 1846. The Kearny Code is too long (113 pages) to include in this small collection. The cover title and one specimen page are reproduced from an inscribed copy of the original presented by Oliver P. Hovey, its printer, to Colonel Doniphan. This copy is now in the Museum of New Mexico. For the somewhat altered text of this code as first reprinted in Washington, see the government document cited above. The most recent authorized edition of the code is found in *New Mexico Statutes 1853, Annotated* (Indianapolis: Allen Smith Co., 1954).

The Treaty of Guadalupe Hidalgo and the Gadsden Treaty are available in English in *New Mexico Statutes 1953, Annotated,* or in equally official bilingual versions published in *New Mexico Statutes, Codification, 1915* (Denver: W.H. Courtright Publishing Co., 1915) and in *Estatutos de Nuevo México, Anotados, Codificación, 1915* (same publisher). The latter was approved by Antonio A. Sedillo, official translator at the time, who was a signer of the New Mexico Constitution in 1911.

The text of the Organic Act separating Arizona from New Mexico was taken from a photocopy of the original, engrossed document signed by President Lincoln.

The English text of the Navajo Treaty of 1868 conforms to the version issued by the Navajo Tribe in *Treaty between the United States of America and the Navajo Tribe of Indians* (Flagstaff: KC Publications, 1968) and to that in *15 Stat. 667.* The text in Navajo was supplied by William Morgan, Sr., and Professor Robert Young, director of the Dictionary Project, Navajo Reading Study, at the University of New Mexico.

Conde's *bando* of 1821, bringing to New Mexico the news of Mexican independence, was typeset in Spanish from a photocopy of the original document provided by Dr. Myra Ellen Jenkins, who also contributed the English translation.

The proclamations of New Mexico governors have been taken directly from photocopies of the original documents in the New Mexico State Records Center and Archives. Proclamations by presidents and the texts of congressional documents have been drawn from various officially approved sources.

The closing document, the Constitution of the State of New Mexico, presents that constitution as amended through mid 1974. In New Mexico amendments and revisions of the Constitution have been incorporated into the original text of the Constitution. This document was provided by Secretary of State Ernestine D. Evans. For extensive annotation and information on court cases and opinions relative to the various sections of the Constitution, the reader is referred to *New Mexico Statutes, 1953, Annotated,* which is cited above.

Special thanks are due a number of individuals who provided prompt and thoughtful assistance. Myron Fink, Law Librarian at the University of New Mexico; Sandra S. Coleman of the Law Library of the University of New Mexico; Edward A. Perkins, Highland High School, Albuquerque; James Purdy, New Mexico State Records Center and Archives; Secretary of State Ernestine D. Evans; Dr. Myra Ellen Jenkins, New Mexico Deputy for Archives and a good friend and respected colleague; and Professor Robert W. Young of the Navajo Reading Study at the University of New Mexico all contributed to the preparation of this volume. I am especially indebted to Jack D. Rittenhouse of the University of New Mexico Press.

Richard N. Ellis
Department of History
University of New Mexico

1

Announcement of Mexico's Independence from Spain, 1821

Isolated New Mexico had not been directly involved in the struggle for Mexican independence that began in 1821, but notification of the successful termination of the struggle signaled numerous changes in the history of New Mexico, not the least of which was the opening of trade with the United States. On August 27, 1821 this *bando* or proclamation was sent by Alejo García Conde, *comandante general* at Chihuahua, to the governor of New Mexico, announcing Mexican independence from Spain.

El Comand^{te} Gral. (Comandante General) de las Provincias Internas de Occidente, á los havitantes de ellas.

Amados compatriotas. Há llegado el dia venturoso destinado por la providencia para que jureis ante los altares la independencia de buestra Patria. El héroe inmortal D^{n} (Don) Agustin de Yturbide y el voto general de los pueblos esplicado del modo mas energico por toda la redondes de la Nueva España, lebanta y consolida á un mismo tiempo el grandioso edificio de buestra libertad. No es posible deciros los bienes que bosotros y principalmente buestros succesores ban á conseguir con esta obra que bendicirá el omnipotente como fundado en los inprescriptibles derechos que concedio á todos los hombres. La Religion santa que profesamos se afiansa del modo mas firme: la justicia es inseparable de unas instituciones que la tienen por fundamento: y las ciencias, la prosperidad del comercio y el progreso de la agricultura y de las artes, son necesariamente los frutos de un Gobierno liberal que se apoya sobre la sana moral y sobre la solida base de la justicia; pero amados compatriotas es necesario que tengais presente que la firme adhesion á las autoridades, la union inseparable de buestros animos, y la mas resuelta determinacion de arrancar de nuestros corasones hasta las mas debiles raises del odio y de la bengansa, son medios indispensables para llegar al alto fin á que aspira la independencia. Sea pues nuestra divisa la Religion, y la mas cordial fraternidad, satisfechos de que la felicidad y progreso duradero de las naciones es solo obra de las virtudes. Chihuagua 27,, de Agosto de 1821.

ALEJO GARCÍA CONDE (Rubric)
(Fran ço) FRANCISCO VELASCO (Rubric)
Sŕio (Secretarío)

1

The Commandant General of the Internal Provinces of the West, to the Inhabitants of them.

Beloved Compatriots. The happy day destined by Providence has arrived wherein you should swear to the independence of our fatherland before the altars. The immortal hero Don Agustin de Yturbide and the general opinion of the people explained in the most energetic form throughout all the confines of New Spain raises, and at the same time solidifies the magnificent edifice of our liberty. It is not possible for us to tell the good things which we, and particularly our successors, are going to carry out with this work which the Almighty will bless as the foundation of the inalienable rights which He gives to all men. The holy religion which we profess is guaranteed in the firmest manner; justice is inseparable from those institutions which have it as their foundation; and the sciences, the prosperity of commerce and the progress of agriculture, and of the arts, are necessarily the fruits of a liberal government which rests upon sane morality and the solid base of justice. But, beloved compatriots, it is necessary that you should bear in mind that the firm adherence to the authorities, the inseparable union of our minds, and the most resolute determination to pull out from our hearts the weakest roots of hatred and of vengeance are the indispensable means in order to reach the high goal to which independence aspires. Inasmuch as religion is our motto as well as the most affectionate brotherhood, we are satisfied that the good fortune and lasting progress of the nations is solely the work of the virtuous. Chihuahua, August 27, 1821.

ALEJO GARCÍA CONDE

FRANCISCO VELASCO
Secretary

Translation by Myra Ellen Jenkins and J. Richard Salazar

2

Proclamation of Stephen W. Kearny upon Entering New Mexico, 1846

Soon after the declaration of war with Mexico, President James K. Polk instructed Colonel Stephen Watts Kearny to conquer New Mexico and California. Kearny's Army of the West, numbering about sixteen hundred men, marched west in small detachments and gathered at Bent's Fort, on the Arkansas River in present-day Colorado, in preparation for the invasion of New Mexico. From his base at Bent's Fort, Kearny sent agents ahead to undermine potential opposition and began issuing a series of statements calculated to obtain the same end. The proclamation of July 31 warned against resistance and promised the protection of the rights of the citizens of New Mexico.

PROCLAMATION OF GENERAL KEARNY, OF 31st JULY

Proclamation to the citizens of New Mexico
by Colonel Kearny
Commanding the United States forces

The undersigned enters New Mexico with a large military force, for the purpose of seeking union with and ameliorating the condition of its inhabitants. This he does under instructions from his government, and with the assurance that he will be amply sustained in the accomplishment of this object. It is enjoined on the citizens of New Mexico to remain quietly at their homes, and to pursue their peaceful avocations. So long as they continue in such pursuits, they will not be interfered with by the American army, but will be respected and protected in their rights, both civil and religious.

All who take up arms or encourage resistance against the government of the United States will be regarded as enemies, and will be treated accordingly.

S.W. KEARNY,
Colonel First Dragoons

CAMP AT BENT'S FORT, ON THE ARKANSAS,
July 31, 1846

3

Proclamation of Stephen W. Kearny upon Occupying Santa Fe, 1846

Following the peaceful occupation of Santa Fe, Kearny, now a brigadier general, made several public statements that expanded upon the previous document. His formal proclamation of August 22, 1846 reiterated the warning against resistance and the promise that the rights of citizens would be protected.

PROCLAMATION BY STEPHEN WATTS KEARNY
Brigadier-General, U.S.A.
Santa Fe, New Mexico, August 22, 1846

PROCLAMATION! As by the act of the Republic of Mexico, a state of war exists between that government and the United States; and as the undersigned, at the head of his troops, on the 18th instant, took possession of Santa Fe, the capital of the department of New Mexico, he now announces his intention to hold the department, with its original boundaries (on both sides of the Del Norte) as a part of the United States, under the name of the Territory of New Mexico.

The undersigned has come to New Mexico with a strong military force, and an equally strong one is following him in the rear. He has more troops than is necessary to put down any opposition that can be brought against him, and therefore it would be but folly or madness for any dissatisfied or discontented persons to think of resisting him.

The undersigned has instructions from his government to respect the religious institutions of New Mexico, to protect the property of the Church, to cause the worship of those belonging to it to be undisturbed, and their religious rights in the amplest manner preserved to them; also to protect the persons and property of all quiet and peaceable inhabitants within its boundaries against their enemies the Eutaws, the Navajos and others; and when he assures all that it will be his pleasure, as well as his duty, to comply with those instructions, he calls upon them to exert themselves in preserving order, in promoting concord, and in maintaining the authority and efficacy of the laws. And he requires of those who have left their homes and taken up arms against the troops of the United States, to return forthwith to them, or else they will be considered as enemies and traitors, subjecting their persons to punishment and their property to seizure and confiscation for the benefit of the public treasury.

It is the wish and intention of the United States to provide for New Mexico a free government, with the least possible delay, similar to those in the United States; and the people of New Mexico will then be called on to exercise the right of freemen in electing their own representatives to the territorial legislature. But, until this can be done, the laws hitherto in force will be continued until changed or modified by competent authority; and those persons holding office will continue in the same for the present, providing they will consider themselves good citizens and are willing to take the oath of allegiance to the United States.

The United States hereby absolves all persons residing within the boundaries of New Mexico from any further allegiance to the Republic of Mexico, and hereby proclaims them citizens of the United States. Those who remain quiet and peaceable will be considered good citizens and receive protection—those who are found in arms, or instigating others against the United States, will be considered traitors and treated accordingly.

Don Manuel Armijo, the late governor of this department, has fled from it; the undersigned has taken possession of it without firing a gun, or spilling a single drop of blood, in which he most truly rejoices, and for the present will be considered as governor of the Territory.

Given at Santa Fe, the capital of the Territory of New Mexico, this 22nd day of August, 1846, and in the 71st year of the independence of the United States.

S.W. KEARNY
Brig. Gen. U.S.A.

By the Governor:
JUAN BAUTISTA VIGIL Y ALARID

4

"Kearny Code": Laws of the Territory of New Mexico, 1846

Eager to establish a government for New Mexico before marching to California, Kearny appointed Captain David Waldo, Private Willard Hall, and Colonel Alexander Doniphan to draft the document that became known as the Kearny Code, which was based on Mexican and American precedents. Soon thereafter Kearny appointed Charles Bent as governor and Antonio José Otero, Carlos Beaubien, and Joab Houghton as territorial judges.

LEYES

DEL

TERRITORIO DE NUEVO MEJICO.

SAÑTA FE, A 7 DE OCTOBRE 1846.

LAWS

OF THE

TERRITORY OF NEW MEXICO.

SANTA FE, OCTOBER 7 1846.

LEYES ORGANICAS

DEL

TERRITORIO

DE

NUEVO MEJICO.

EL Gobierno de los Estados Unidos de America ordena y establece las siguientes leyes organicas para el Territorio de Nuevo Mejico que ha sido hecho un Territorio de dicho Gobierno.

ARTÍCULO 1º.

[*Poder ejecutivo.*]

SECION 1 a.—EL pais antes conocido por Nuevo Mejico será conocido y designado de aqui en adelante por el Territorio de Nuevo Mejico en los Estados Unidos de America, y el gobierno provisional de dicho Territorio será organizado segun aqui se prescribe.

ARTICULO 2º.

[*Poder ejecutivo.*]

SECION 1 a.—EL poder ejecutivo será confiado á un Gobernador que será es elidido Poncern y que

---

ORGANIC LAW

OF THE

TERRITORY

OF

NEW MEXICO

The government of the United States of America, ordains and establishes, the following organic law for the Territory of said government.

ARTICLE I.

SEC. 1. The country heretofore known as New Mexico shall be known and hereafter designated as the territory of New Mexico in the United States of America, and the temporary government of the said territory shall be organized and administered in the manner hereinafter prescribed.

ARTICLE 2.

Executive Power.

SEC. 1. The Executive power shall be vested in a Governor, who shall es elin the est. Perstar, na snal

5

Bill of Rights, from Kearny Code, 1846

The establishment of a new government by Kearny signified major changes in New Mexico political life, but nowhere was this more evident than in the Bill of Rights. Patterned after the Bill of Rights in the United States Constitution, this portion of the Kearny Code provided the protection of individual rights that United States citizens had come to expect but which were unfamiliar to former citizens of New Spain and Mexico. It was important, then, in the Americanization of this new acquisition.

BILL OF RIGHTS
As Declared By
BRIGADIER GENERAL STEPHEN W. KEARNY

September 22, 1846

That the great and essential principles of liberty and free government may be recognized and established it is hereby declared:

First. That all political power is vested in and belongs to the people.

Second. That the people have the right peaceably to assemble for their common good, and to apply to those in power for redress of grievances by petition or remonstrance.

Third. That all men have a natural indefeasible right to worship Almighty God according to the dictates of their own conscience; that no person can ever be hurt, molested, or restrained in his religious professions if he do not disturb others in their religious worship; and that all Christian churches shall be protected and none oppressed, and that no person on account of his religious opinions shall be rendered ineligible to any office of honor, trust or profit.

Fourth. The courts of justice shall be open to every person; just remedy given for every injury to person or property, and that right and justice shall be administered without sale, denial, or delay, and that no private property shall be taken for public use without just compensation.

Fifth. The right of trial by jury shall remain inviolate.

Sixth. In all criminal cases the accused has the right to be heard by himself and counsel, to demand the nature and cause of the accusations, to have compulsory process for witnesses in his favor, to meet the witnesses against him face to face, and to have a speedy trial by a jury of his county.

Seventh. The accused cannot be compelled to give evidence against himself, or be deprived of life, liberty, or property but by a verdict of a jury and the laws of the land.

Eighth. No person after having once been acquitted by a jury can be tried a second time for the same offense.

Ninth. That all persons shall be bailed by sufficient sureties, except in capital offenses where proof of guilt is evident, and the privileges of a writ of habeas corpus cannot be suspended except the public safety shall require it in the case of rebellion or invasion.

Tenth. Excessive bail shall not be required, excessive fines imposed, nor cruel and unusual punishment inflicted.

Eleventh. The people shall be secure in their persons, papers, houses and effects from unreasonable searches and seizures, and that no writ shall issue for a search or seizure without a probable cause of guilt is made out under oath.

Twelfth. That free communication of thoughts and opinions is one of the inviolable rights of freemen, and that every person may freely speak, write, or print on any subject, being responsible for every abuse of that liberty.

Thirteenth. That no vicar, priest, preacher of the gospel, nor teacher of any religious denomination shall ever be compelled to bear arms, or to serve on juries, work on roads, or perform military duty.

Done at the government house, in the City of Santa Fe, in the Territory of New Mexico, by Brigadier General Stephen W. Kearny, by virtue of the authority conferred upon him by the government of the United States, this twenty-second day of September, A.D. 1846.

S.W. KEARNY,
Brig. Gen. U.S.A.

6

Treaty of Guadalupe Hidalgo, 1848

The man designated by President Polk to negotiate the end of the Mexican War was Nicholas Trist, chief clerk of the Department of State. Trist's efforts failed until after General Winfield Scott captured Mexico City. Trist himself was recalled by the president but decided to violate his instructions because the opportunity to conclude a treaty had presented itself. Although Polk was annoyed, he decided to recommend ratification of the treaty because of growing opposition to the war.

TREATY OF PEACE
between the
UNITED STATES AND MEXICO

Executed at the City of Guadalupe Hidalgo, February 2, 1848
Ratification exchanged at Queretaro, May 30, 1848. Proclamation made
July 4, 1848

In the Name of Almighty God:
  The United States of America and the united Mexican states, animated by a sincere desire to put an end to the calamities of the war which unhappily exists between the two republics, and to establish upon a solid basis relations of peace and friendship, which shall confer reciprocal benefits upon the citizens of both, and assure the concord, harmony, and mutual confidence wherein the two people should live, as good neighbors, have for that purpose appointed their respective plenipotentiaries—that is to say, the President of the United States has appointed Nicholas P. Trist, a citizen of the United States, and the President of the Mexican republic has appointed Don Luis Gonzaga Cuevas, Don Bernardo Couto, and Don Miguel Atristain, citizens of the said republic, who, after a reciprocal communication of their respective full powers, have, under the protection of Almighty God, the Author of Peace, arranged, agreed upon, and signed the following

TREATY OF PEACE, FRIENDSHIP, LIMITS, AND SETTLEMENT BETWEEN
THE UNITED STATES OF AMERICA AND THE MEXICAN REPUBLIC

ARTICLE I

There shall be firm and universal peace between the United States of America and the Mexican republic, and between their respective countries, territories, cities, towns, and people, without exception of places or persons.

10

ARTICLE II

Immediately upon the signature of this treaty, a convention shall be entered into between a commissioner or commissioners appointed by the general-in-chief of the forces of the United States, and such as may be appointed by the Mexican government, to the end that a provisional suspension of hostilities shall take place, and that, in the places occupied by the said forces, constitutional order may be re-established, as regards the political, administrative, and judicial branches, so far as this shall be permitted by the circumstances of military occupation.

ARTICLE III

Immediately upon the ratification of the present treaty by the government of the United States, orders shall be transmitted to the commanders of their land and naval forces, requiring the latter (provided this treaty shall then have been ratified by the government of the Mexican republic, and the ratifications exchanged) immediately to desist from blockading any Mexican ports; and requiring the former (under the same condition) to commence, at the earliest moment practicable, withdrawing all troops of the United States then in the interior of the Mexican republic, to points that shall be selected by common agreement, at a distance from the seaports not exceeding thirty leagues; and such evacuation of the interior of the republic shall be completed with the least possible delay; the Mexican government hereby binding itself to afford every facility in its power for rendering the same convenient to the troops, on their march and in their new positions, and for promoting a good understanding between them and the inhabitants. In like manner orders shall be dispatched to the persons in charge of the custom-houses at all ports occupied by the forces of the United States, requiring them (under the same condition) immediately to deliver possession of the same to the persons authorized by the Mexican government to receive it, together with all bonds and evidences of debt for duties on importations and on exportations, not yet fallen due. Moreover, a faithful and exact account shall be made out, showing the entire amount of all duties on imports and on exports, collected at such custom-houses, or elsewhere in Mexico, by authority of the United States, from and after the day of the ratification of this treaty by the government of the Mexican republic; and also an account of the cost of collection; and such entire amount, deducting only the cost of collection, shall be delivered to the Mexican government, at the City of Mexico, within three months after the exchange of ratifications.

The evacuation of the capital of the Mexican republic by the troops of the United States, in virtue of the above stipulation, shall be completed in one month after the orders there stipulated for shall have been received by the commander of said troops, or sooner if possible.

ARTICLE IV

Immediately after the exchange of ratifications of the present treaty, all castles, forts, territories, places, and possessions, which have been taken or occupied by the forces of the United States during the present war, within the limits of the Mexican republic, as about to be established by the following article, shall be definitely restored to the said republic, together with all the artillery, arms, apparatus of war, munitions, and other public property, which were in the said castles and forts when captured, and which shall remain there at the time when this treaty shall be duly ratified by the government of the

Mexican republic. To this end, immediately upon the signature of this treaty, orders shall be dispatched to the American officers commanding such castles and forts, securing against the removal or destruction of any such artillery, arms, apparatus of war, munitions, or other public property. The City of Mexico, within the inner line of entrenchments surrounding the said city, is comprehended in the above stipulations, as regards the restoration of artillery, apparatus of war, etc.

The final evacuation of the territory of the Mexican republic, by the forces of the United States, shall be completed in three months from the said exchange of ratifications, or sooner if possible: The Mexican, government hereby engaging, as in the foregoing article, to use all means in its power for facilitating such evacuation, and rendering it convenient to the troops, and for promoting a good understanding between them and the inhabitants.

If, however, the ratification of this treaty by both parties should not take place in time to allow the embarkation of the troops of the United States to be completed before the commencement of the sickly season, at the Mexican ports on the Gulf of Mexico, in such case a friendly arrangement shall be entered into between the general-in-chief of the said troops and the Mexican government, whereby healthy and otherwise suitable places, at a distance from the ports not exceeding thirty leagues, shall be designated for the residence of such troops as may not yet have embarked, until the return of the healthy season. And the space of time here referred to as comprehending the sickly season, shall be understood to extend from the first day of May to the first day of November.

All prisoners of war taken on either side, on land or on sea, shall be restored as soon as practicable after the exchange of ratifications of this treaty. It is also agreed that if any Mexicans should now be held as captives by any savage tribe within the limits of the United States, as about to be established by the following article, the government of the said United States will exact the release of such captives, and cause them to be restored to their country.

ARTICLE V

The boundary line between the two republics shall commence in the Gulf of Mexico, three leagues from land, opposite the mouth of the Rio Grande, otherwise called Rio Bravo del Norte, or opposite the mouth of its deepest branch, if it should have more than one branch emptying directly into the sea; from thence up the middle of that river, following the deepest channel, where it has more than one, to the point where it strikes the southern boundary of New Mexico; thence, westwardly, along the whole southern boundary of New Mexico (which runs north of the town called Paso) to its western termination; thence, northward, along the western line of New Mexico, until it intersects the first branch of the river Gila; (or if it should not intersect any branch of that river, then to the point on the said line nearest to such branch, and thence in a direct line to the same;) thence down the middle of the said branch and of the said river, until it empties into the Rio Colorado; thence across the Rio Colorado, following the division line between Upper and Lower California, to the Pacific Ocean.

The southern and western limits of New Mexico, mentioned in this article, are those laid down in the map entitled "Map of the United Mexican States, as organized and defined by various acts of the Congress of said republic, and constructed according to the best authorities. Revised edition. Published at New York, in 1847, by J. Disturnell." Of which map a copy is added to this treaty, bearing the signatures and seals of the undersigned plenipotentiaries. And, in order to preclude all difficulty in tracing upon the ground the limit separating Upper from Lower California, it is agreed that the said limit shall consist of a straight line drawn from the middle of the Rio Gila, where it unites with the Colorado, to a point on the coast of the Pacific Ocean distant one marine league due south of the southernmost point of the port of San Diego, according to the plan of said port made in the year 1782 by Don Juan Pantoja, second sailing-master of the Spanish fleet, and published at Madrid in the year 1802, in the atlas to the voyage of the schooners Sutil and Mexicana, of which plan a copy is hereunto added, signed and sealed by the respective plenipotentiaries.

In order to designate the boundary line with due precision, upon authoritative maps, and to establish upon the ground landmarks which shall show the limits of both republics, as described in the present article, the two governments shall each appoint a commissioner and a surveyor, who, before the expiration of one year from the date of the exchange of ratifications of this treaty, shall meet at the port of San Diego, and proceed to run and mark the said boundary in its whole course to the mouth of the Rio Bravo del Norte. They shall keep journals and make out plans of their operations; and the result agreed upon by them shall be deemed a part of this treaty, and shall have the same force as if it were inserted therein. The two governments will amicably agree regarding what may be necessary to these persons, and also as to their respective escorts, should such be necessary.

The boundary line established by this article shall be religiously respected by each of the two republics, and no change shall ever be made therein, except by the express and free consent of both nations, lawfully given by the general government of each, in conformity with its own Constitution.

ARTICLE VI

The vessels and citizens of the United States shall, in all time, have a free and uninterrupted passage by the Gulf of California, and by the river Colorado below its confluence with the Gila, to and from their possessions situated north of the boundary line defined in the preceding article; it being understood that this passage is to be by navigating the Gulf of California and the river Colorado, and not by land, without the express consent of the Mexican government.

If, by the examinations which may be made, it should be ascertained to be practicable and advantageous to construct a road, canal, or railway, which should in whole or in part run upon the river Gila, or upon its right or its left bank, within the space of one marine league from either margin of the river, the governments of both republics will form an agreement regarding its construction, in order that it may serve equally for the use and advantage of both countries.

ARTICLE VII

The river Gila, and the part of the Rio Bravo del Norte lying below the southern boundary of New Mexico, being, agreeably to the fifth article, divided in the middle between the two republics, the navigation of the Gila and of the Bravo below said boundary shall be free and common to the vessels and citizens of both countries; and neither shall, without the consent of the other, construct any work that may impede or interrupt, in whole or in part, the exercise of this right; not even for the purpose of favoring new methods of navigation. Nor shall any tax or contribution, under any denomination or title, be levied upon vessels, or persons navigating the same, or upon merchandise or effects transported thereon, except in the case of landing upon one of their shores. If, for the purpose of making the said rivers navigable, or for maintaining them in such state, it should be necessary or advantageous to establish any tax or contribution, this shall not be done without the consent of both governments.

The stipulations contained in the present article shall not impair the territorial rights of either republic within its established limits.

ARTICLE VIII

Mexicans now established in territories previously belonging to Mexico, and which remain for the future within the limits of the United States, as defined by the present treaty, shall be free to continue where they now reside, or to remove at any time to the Mexican republic, retaining the property which they possess in the said territories, or disposing thereof, and removing the proceeds wherever they please, without their being subjected, on this account, to any contribution, tax, or charge whatever.

Those who shall prefer to remain in the said territories, may either retain the title and rights of Mexican citizens, or acquire those of citizens of the United States. But they shall be under the obligation to make their election within one year from the date of the exchange of ratifications of this treaty; and those who shall remain in the said territories after the expiration of that year, without having declared their intention to retain the character of Mexicans, shall be considered to have elected to become citizens of the United States.

In the said territories, property of every kind, now belonging to Mexicans not established there, shall be inviolably respected. The present owners, the heirs of these, and all Mexicans who may hereafter acquire said property by contract, shall enjoy with respect to it guaranties equally ample as if the same belonged to citizens of the United States.

ARTICLE IX

Mexicans who, in the territories aforesaid, shall not preserve the character of citizens of the Mexican republic, conformably with what is stipulated in the preceding article, shall be incorporated into the Union of the United States, and be admitted at the proper time (to be judged of by the Congress of the United States) to the enjoyment of all the rights of citizens of the United States, according to the principles of the Constitution; and in the meantime shall be maintained and protected in the free enjoyment of their liberty and property, and secured in the free exercise of their religion without restriction.

ARTICLE X
(Stricken out)

ARTICLE XI

Considering that a great part of the territories which, by the present treaty, are to be comprehended for the future within the limits of the United States, is now occupied by savage tribes, who will hereafter be under the exclusive control of the government of the United States, and whose incursions within the territory of Mexico would be prejudicial in the extreme, it is solemnly agreed that all such incursions shall be forcibly restrained by the government of the United States whensoever this may be necessary; and that when they cannot be prevented, they shall be punished by the said government, and satisfaction for the same shall be exacted—all in the same way, and with equal diligence and energy, as if the same incursions were meditated or committed within its own territory, against its own citizens.

It shall not be lawful, under any pretext whatever, for any inhabitant of the United States to purchase or acquire any Mexican, or any foreigner residing in Mexico, who may have been captured by Indians inhabiting the territory of either of the two republics, nor to purchase or acquire horses, mules, cattle, or property of any kind, stolen within Mexican territory by such Indians.

And in the event of any person or persons, captured within Mexican territory by Indians, being carried into the territory of the United States, the government of the latter engages and binds itself, in the most solemn manner, so soon as it shall know of such captives being within its territory, and shall be able so to do, through the faithful exercise of its influence and power, to rescue them and return them to their country, or deliver them to the agent or representative of the Mexican government. The Mexican authorities will, as far as practicable, give to the government of the United States notice of such captures; and its agent shall pay the expenses incurred in the maintenance and transmission of the rescued captives; who, in the meantime, shall be treated with the utmost hospitality by the American authorities at the place where they may be. But if the government of the United States, before receiving such notice from Mexico, should obtain intelligence, through any other channel, of the existence of Mexican captives within its territory, it will proceed forthwith to effect their release and delivery to the Mexican agent, as above stipulated.

For the purpose of giving to these stipulations the fullest possible efficacy, thereby affording the security and redress demanded by their true spirit and intent, the government of the United States will now and hereafter pass, without unnecessary delay, and always vigilantly enforce, such laws as the nature of the subject may require. And finally, the sacredness of this obligation shall never be lost sight of by the said government when providing for the removal of the Indians from any portion of the said territories, or for its being settled by citizens of the United States; but on the contrary, special care shall then be taken not to place its Indian occupants under the necessity of seeking new homes, by committing those invasions which the United States have solemnly obligated themselves to restrain.

ARTICLE XII

In consideration of the extension acquired by the boundaries of the United States, as defined in the fifth article of the present treaty, the government of the United States engages to pay to that of the Mexican republic the sum of fifteen millions of dollars.

Immediately after this treaty shall have been duly ratified by the government of the Mexican republic, the sum of three millions of dollars shall be paid to the said government by that of the United States, at the City of Mexico, in the gold or silver coin of Mexico. The remaining twelve millions of dollars shall be paid at the same place, and in the same coin, in annual instalments of three millions of dollars each, together with interest on the same at the rate of six per centum per annum. This interest shall begin to run upon the whole sum of twelve millions from the day of the ratification of the present treaty by the Mexican government, and the first of the instalments shall be paid at the expiration of one year from the same day. Together with each annual instalment, as it falls due, the whole interest accruing on such instalment from the beginning shall also be paid.

ARTICLE XIII

The United States engage, moreover, to assume and pay to the claimants all the amounts now due them, and those hereafter to become due, by reason of the claims already liquidated and decided against the Mexican republic, under the conventions between the two republics severally concluded on the eleventh day of April, eighteen hundred and thirty-nine, and on the thirtieth day of January, eighteen hundred and forty-three; so that the Mexican republic shall be absolutely exempt, for the future, from all expense whatever on account of the said claims.

ARTICLE XIV

The United States do furthermore discharge the Mexican republic from all claims of citizens of the United States, not heretofore decided against the Mexican government, which may have arisen previously to the date of the signature of this treaty; which discharge shall be final and perpetual, whether the said claims be rejected or be allowed by the board of commissioners provided for in the following article, and whatever shall be the total amount of those allowed.

ARTICLE XV

The United States, exonerating Mexico from all demands on account of the claims of their citizens mentioned in the preceding article, and considering them entirely and forever canceled, whatever their amount may be, undertake to make satisfaction for the same, to an amount not exceeding three and one-quarter millions of dollars. To ascertain the validity and amount of those claims, a board of commissioners shall be established by the government of the United States, whose awards shall be final and conclusive: Provided, That in deciding upon the validity of each claim, the board shall be guided and governed by the principles and rules of decision prescribed by the first and fifth articles of the unratified convention, concluded at the City of Mexico on the twentieth day of November, one thousand eight hundred and forty-three; and in no case shall an award be made in favor of any claim not embraced by these principles and rules.

If, in the opinion of the said board of commissioners, or of the claimants, any books, records, or documents in the possession or power of the government of the Mexican republic, shall be deemed necessary to the just decision of any claim, the commissioners, or the claimants through them, shall, within such period as Congress may designate, make an application in writing for the same, addressed to the Mexican minister for foreign affairs, to be transmitted by the secretary of state of the United States; and the Mexican government engages, at the earliest possible moment after the receipt of such demand, to cause any of the books, records, or documents, so specified, which shall be in their possession or power, (or authenticated copies or extracts of the same,) to be transmitted to the said secretary of state, who shall immediately deliver them over to the said board of commissioners: Provided, That no such application shall be made by, or at the instance of, any claimant, until the facts which it is expected to prove by such books, records, or documents, shall have been stated under oath or affirmation.

ARTICLE XVI

Each of the contracting parties reserves to itself the entire right to fortify whatever point within its territory it may judge proper so to fortify, for its security.

ARTICLE XVII

The treaty of amity, commerce, and navigation, concluded at the City of Mexico on the fifth day of April, A.D. 1831, between the United States of America and the united Mexican states, except the additional article, and except so far as the stipulations of the said treaty may be incompatible with any stipulation contained in the present treaty, is hereby revived for the period of eight years from the day of the exchange of ratifications of this treaty, with the same force and virtue as if incorporated therein; it being understood that each of the contracting parties reserves to itself the right, at any time after the said period of eight years shall have expired, to terminate the same by giving one year's notice of such intention to the other party.

ARTICLE XVIII

All supplies whatever for troops of the United States in Mexico, arriving at ports in the occupation of such troops previous to the final evacuation thereof, although subsequently to the restoration of the custom-houses at such ports, shall be entirely exempt from duties and charges of any kind; the government of the United States hereby engaging and pledging its faith to establish, and vigilantly to enforce, all possible guards for securing the revenue of Mexico, by preventing the importation, under cover of this stipulation, of any articles other than such, both in kind and in quantity, as shall really be wanted for the use and consumption of the forces of the United States during the time they may remain in Mexico. To this end, it shall be the duty of all officers and agents of the United States to denounce to the Mexican authorities at the respective ports any attempts at a fraudulent abuse of this stipulation which they may know of or may have reason to suspect, and to give to such authorities all the aid in their power with regard thereto; and every such attempt, when duly proved and established by sentence of a competent tribunal, shall be punished by the confiscation of the property so attempted to be fraudulently introduced.

ARTICLE XIX

With respect to all merchandise, effects, and property whatsoever, imported into ports of Mexico whilst in the occupation of the forces of the United States, whether by citizens of either republic, or by citizens or subjects of any neutral nation, the following rules shall be observed:—

1. All such merchandise, effects, and property, if imported previously to the restoration of the custom-houses to the Mexican authorities, as stipulated for in the third article of this treaty, shall be exempt from confiscation, although the importation of the same be prohibited by the Mexican tariff.

2. The same perfect exemption shall be enjoyed by all such merchandise, effects, and property, imported subsequently to the restoration of the

custom-houses, and previously to the sixty days fixed in the following article for the coming into force of the Mexican tariff at such ports respectively; the said merchandise, effects, and property being, however, at the time of their importation, subject to the payment of duties, as provided for in the said following article.

3. All merchandise, effects, and property described in the two rules foregoing shall, during their continuance at the place of importation, and upon their leaving such place for the interior, be exempt from all duty, tax, or impost of every kind, under whatsoever title or denomination. Nor shall they be there subjected to any charge whatsoever upon the sale thereof.

4. All merchandise, effects, and property, described in the first and second rules, which shall have been removed to any place in the interior whilst such place was in the occupation of the forces of the United States, shall, during their continuance therein, be exempt from all tax upon the sale or consumption thereof, and from every kind of impost or contribution, under whatsoever title or denomination.

5. But if any merchandise, effects, or property, described in the first and second rules, shall be removed to any place not occupied at the time by the forces of the United States, they shall, upon their introduction into such place, or upon their sale or consumption there, be subject to the same duties which, under the Mexican laws, they would be required to pay in such cases if they had been imported in time of peace, through the maritime custom-houses, and had there paid the duties conformably with the Mexican tariff.

6. The owners of all merchandise, effects, or property described in the first and second rules, and existing in any port of Mexico, shall have the right to reship the same, exempt from all tax, impost, or contribution whatever.

With respect to the metals, or other property, exported from any Mexican port whilst in the occupation of the forces of the United States, and previously to the restoration of the custom-house at such port, no person shall be required by the Mexican authorities, whether general or state, to pay any tax, duty, or contribution upon any such exportation, or in any manner to account for the same to the said authorities.

ARTICLE XX

Through consideration for the interests of commerce generally, it is agreed, that if less than sixty days should elapse between the date of the signature of this treaty and the restoration of the custom-houses, conformably with the stipulation in the third article, in such case all merchandise, effects, and property whatsoever, arriving at the Mexican ports after the restoration of the said custom-houses, and previously to the expiration of sixty days after the day of the signature of this treaty, shall be admitted to entry; and no other duties shall be levied thereon than the duties established by the tariff found in force at such custom-houses at the time of the restoration of the same. And to all such merchandise, effects, and property, the rules established by the preceding article shall apply.

ARTICLE XXI

If unhappily any disagreement should hereafter arise between the governments of the two republics, whether with respect to the interpretation of any stipulation in this treaty, or with respect to any other particular concerning the political or commercial relations of the two nations, the said governments, in the name of those nations, do promise to each other that they will endeavor, in the most sincere and earnest manner, to settle the differences so arising, and to preserve the state of peace and friendship in which the two countries are now placing themselves; using, for this end, mutual representations and specific negotiations. And if, by these means, they should not be enabled to come to an agreement, a resort shall not, on this account, be had to reprisals, aggression, or hostility of any kind, by the one republic against the other, until the government of that which deems itself aggrieved shall have maturely considered, in the spirit of peace and good neighborship, whether it would not be better that such difference should be settled by the arbitration of commissioners appointed on each side, or by that of a friendly nation. And should such course be proposed by either party, it shall be acceded to by the other, unless deemed by it altogether incompatible with the nature of the difference, or the circumstances of the case.

ARTICLE XXII

If (which is not to be expected, and which God forbid!) war should unhappily break out between the two republics, they do now, with a view to such calamity, solemnly pledge themselves to each other and to the world, to observe the following rules; absolutely where the nature of the subject permits, and as closely as possible in all cases where such absolute observance shall be impossible:—

1. The merchants of either republic then residing in the other shall be allowed to remain twelve months, (for those dwelling in the interior,) and six months (for those dwelling at the seaports,) to collect their debts and settle their affairs; during which periods, they shall enjoy the same protection, and be on the same footing, in all respects, as the citizens or subjects of the most friendly nations; and, at the expiration thereof, or at any time before, they shall have full liberty to depart, carrying off all their effects without molestation or hindrance, conforming therein to the same laws which the citizens or subjects of the most friendly nations are required to conform to. Upon the entrance of the armies of either nation into the territories of the other, women and children, ecclesiastics, scholars of every faculty, cultivators of the earth, merchants, artisans, manufacturers, and fishermen, unarmed and inhabiting unfortified towns, villages, or places, and in general all persons whose occupations are for the common subsistence and benefit of mankind, shall be allowed to continue their respective employments unmolested in their persons. Nor shall their houses or goods be burnt or otherwise destroyed, nor their cattle taken, nor their fields wasted, by the armed force into whose power, by the events of war, they may happen to fall; but if the necessity arise to take anything from them for the use of such armed force, the same shall be paid for at an equitable price. All churches, hospitals, schools, colleges, libraries, and other establishments for charitable and beneficent purposes, shall be respected, and all persons connected with the same protected in the discharge of their duties, and the pursuit of their vocations.

2. In order that the fate of prisoners of war may be alleviated, all such practices as those of sending them into distant inclement or unwholesome districts, or crowding them into close and noxious places, shall be studiously avoided. They shall not be confined in dungeons, prison ships, or prisons; nor be put in irons, or bound, or otherwise restrained in the use of their limbs. The officers shall enjoy liberty on their paroles, within convenient districts, and have comfortable quarters; and the common soldiers shall be disposed in cantonments, open and extensive enough for air and exercise, and lodged in barracks as roomy and good as are provided by the party in whose power they

are for its own troops. But if any officer shall break his parole by leaving the district so assigned him, or any other prisoner shall escape from the limits of his cantonment, after they shall have been designated to him, such individual, officer, or other prisoner, shall forfeit so much of the benefit of this article as provides for his liberty on parole or in cantonment. And if any officer so breaking his parole, or any common soldier so escaping from the limits assigned him, shall afterwards be found in arms, previously to his being regularly exchanged, the person so offending shall be dealt with according to the established laws of war. The officers shall be daily furnished by the party in whose power they are, with as many rations, and of the same articles, as are allowed, either in kind or by commutation, to officers of equal rank in its own army; and all others shall be daily furnished with such ration as is allowed to a common soldier in its own service: The value of all which supplies shall, at the close of the war, or at periods to be agreed upon between the respective commanders, be paid by the other party, on a mutual adjustment of accounts for the subsistence of prisoners; and such accounts shall not be mingled with or set off against any others, nor the balance due on them be withheld, as a compensation or reprisal for any cause whatever, real or pretended. Each party shall be allowed to keep a commissary of prisoners, appointed by itself, with every cantonment of prisoners, in possession of the other; which commissary shall see the prisoners as often as he pleases; shall be allowed to receive, exempt from all duties or taxes, and to distribute, whatever comforts may be sent to them by their friends; and shall be free to transmit his reports in open letters to the party by whom he is employed.

And it is declared that neither the pretense that war dissolves all treaties, nor any other whatever, shall be considered as annulling or suspending the solemn covenant contained in this article. On the contrary, the state of war is precisely that for which it is provided; and during which, its stipulations are to be as sacredly observed as the most acknowledged obligations under the law of nature or nations.

ARTICLE XXIII

This treaty shall be ratified by the President of the United States of America, by and with the advice and consent of the senate thereof; by the President of the Mexican republic, with the previous approbation of its general congress; and the ratifications shall be exchanged in the city of Washington, or at the seat of government of Mexico, in four months from the date of the signature hereof, or sooner if practicable.

In faith whereof, we, the respective plenipotentiaries, have signed this treaty of peace, friendship, limits, and settlement; and have hereunto affixed our seals respectively. Done in quintuplicate, at the city of Guadalupe Hidalgo, on the second day of February, in the year of our Lord one thousand eight hundred and forty-eight.

N.P. TRIST,
LUIS G. CUEVAS,
BERNARDO COUTO,
MIGL. ATRISTAIN.

TRATADO DE PAZ

entre los

ESTADOS UNIDOS Y MEXICO

EJECUTADO EN

LA CIUDAD DE GUADALUPE HIDALGO,

FEBRERO 2, 1848.

Ratificacion cambiada en Querétaro, Mayo 30 de 1848. Proclama hecha Julio 4 de 1848.

En El Nombre de Dios Todo Poderoso:

Los Estados Unidos Méxicanos y los Estados Unidos de América, animados de un sincéro deseo de poner término a las calamidades de la guerra que desgraciadamente existen entre ambas repúblicas, y de establecer sobre bases sólidas relaciones de paz y buena amistad, que procuren recíprocas ventajas a los ciudadanos de uno y otro país, y afianzen la concordia, armonía y mútua seguridad en que deben vivir, como buenos vecinos, los dos pueblos han nombrado a éste efecto sus respectivos plenipontenciarios; a saber: El Presidente de la República Méxicana a Don Bernardo Couto, Don Miguel Atristain, y Don Luis Gonzaga Cuevas, ciudadanos de la misma república; y el Presidente de los Estados Unidos de America a Don Nicolás P. Trist, ciudadano de dichos estados; quienes después de haberse comunicado sus plenos poderes bajo la proteccion del Señor Dios Todo Poderoso, autor de la paz, han ajustado, convenido, y firmado el siguiente:

TRATADO DE PAZ, AMISTAD, LIMITES Y ARREGLO DEFINITIVO ENTRE LA REPUBLICA MEXICANA Y LOS ESTADOS UNIDOS DE AMERICA.

ARTICULO I

Habrá paz firme y universal entre la República Méxicana y los Estados Unidos de América, y entre sus respectivos países, territorios, ciudades, villas y pueblos, sin excepcion de lugares o personas.

ARTICULO II

Luego que se fírme el presente tratado, habrá un convenio entre el comisionado u comisionados del gobierno Méxicano, y él, o los que nombre el general en jefe de las fuerzas de los Estados Unidos, para que cesen provisionalmente las hostilidades, y se restablezca en los lugares ocupados por las mismas fuerzas el órden constitucional en lo político, administrativo, y judicial, en cuanto lo permitan las circunstancias de ocupacion militar.

ARTICULO III

Luego que éste tratado sea ratificado por el gobierno de los Estados Unidos, se expedirán órdenes a sus comandantes de tierra y mar previniendo a éstos segundos (siempre que el tratado haya sido ya ratificado por el gobierno de la República Mexicana y canjeadas las ratificaciones), que inmediatamente alcen el bloqueo de todos los puertos Méxicanos, y mandando a los primeros (bajo la misma condicion) que a la mayor posible brevedad comienzen a retirar todas las tropas de los Estados Unidos que se hallaren entónces en el interior de la República Méxicana, a puntos que se elegirán de común acuerdo, y que no distarán de los puertos más de treinta leguas; ésta evacuacion del interior de la república se consumará con la menor dilacion posible, comprometiéndose a la vez el gobierno Méxicano a facilitar, cuanto quepa en su arbitrio, la evacuacion de las tropas Americanas; a hacer cómoda su marcha y su permanencia en los nuevos puntos que se elijan; y a promover una buena inteligencia entre ellos y los habitantes. Igualmente se librarán órdenes a las personas encargadas de las aduanas marítimas en todos los puertos ocupados por las fuerzas de los Estados Unidos, previniéndoles (bajo la misma condicion) que pongan inmediatamente en posesión de dichas aduanas a las personas autorizadas por el gobierno Méxicano para recibirlas, entregándoles al mismo tiempo todas las obligaciones y constancias de deudas pendientes por derechos de importacion y exportacion, cuyos plazos no estén vencidos. Además se formará una cuenta fiel y exacta que manifeste el total monto de los derechos de importacion y exportacion, recaudados en las mismas aduanas marítimas o en cualquiera otro lugar de México por autoridad de los Estados Unidos desde el día de la ratificacion de éste tratado por el gobierno de la República Méxicana; y tambien una cuenta de los gastos de recaudacion; y la total suma de los derechos cotrados, deducidos solamente los gastos de recaudacion, se entregará al gobierno Méxicano en la ciudad de México a los tres mesas del canje de las ratificaciones.

La evacuacion de la capital de la República Méxicana por las tropas de los Estados Unidos, en consecuencia de lo que queda estipulado, se completará al mes de recibirse por el comandante de dichas tropas las órdenes convenidas en el presente artículo, o antes si fuere posible.

ARTICULO IV

Luego que se verifíque el canje de las ratificaciones del presente tratado, todos los castillos, fortalezas, territorios, lugares y posesiones que hayan tomado u ocupado las fuerzas de los Estados Unidos, en la presente guerra, dentro de los límites que por el siguiente artículo van a fijarse a la República Méxicana, se devolverán definitivamente a la misma república, con toda la artillería, armas, aparejos de guerra, municiones, y cualquiera otra propiedad pública existentes en dichos castillos y fortalezas, cuando fueron tomados, y que se conserve en ellos al tiempo de ratificarse por el gobierno de la República Méxicana el presente tratado. A éste efecto, inmediatamente después que se fírme, se expedirán órdenes a los oficiales Americanos que mandan dichos castillos y fortalezas para asegurar toda la artillería, armas, aparejos de guerra, municiones, y cualquiera otra propiedad pública, la cual no podrá en adelante removerse de donde se halla, ni destruirse. La Ciudad de México dentro de la línea interior de atrincheramientos que la circundan queda comprendida en la precedente estipulacion en lo que toca a la devolucion de artillería, aparejos de guerra, etc.

La final evacuacion del Territorio de la República Mexicana por las fuerzas de los Estados Unidos quedará consumada a los tres meses, del canje de las ratificaciones, o ántes si fuere posible, comprometiéndose a la vez el gobierno Mexicano, como en el artículo anterior a usar de todos los medios que estén en su poder para facilitar la tal evacuacion, hacerla cómodo a las tropas Americanas, y promover entre ellas y los habitantes una buena inteligencia.

Sinembargo, si la ratificacion del presente tratado por ambas partes no tuviera efecto en tiempo que permita que el embarque de las tropas de los Estados Unidos se complete, ántes de que comienze la estacion mal sana en los puertos Mexicanos del Golfo de México; en tal caso, se hará un arreglo amistoso entre el gobierno Méxicano y el general en jefe de dichas tropas, y por medio de, éste arreglo se señalarán lugares salubres y convenientes, (que no disten de los puertos más de treinta leguas), para que residan en ellos hasta la vuelta de la estacion sana las tropas que aún no se hay an embarcado. Y queda entendido que el especio de tiempo de que aquí se habla, como comprehensivo de la estacion mal sana, se extiende desde el día primero de Mayo hasta el día primero de Noviembre.

Todos los prisioneros de guerra tomados en mar o tierra por ambas partes, se restituirán a la mayor brevedad posible después del canje de las ratificaciones del presente tratado. Queda también convenido que si algunos Mexicanos estubiéren ahora cautivos en poder de alguna tríbu salvaje dentro de los límites que por el siguiente artículo van a fijarse a los Estados Unidos el gobierno de los mismos Estados Unidos exigirá su libertad y los hará restituir a su país.

ARTICULO V

La línea divisoria entre las dos repúblicas comenzará en el Golfo de México; tres leguas fuera de tierra frente a la desembocadura del Rio Grande, llamado por otro nombre Rio Bravo del Norte; o del más profundo de sus brazos, si en la desembocadura tuviere varios brazos; correrá por mitad de dicho rio, siguiendo el canal más profundo, donde tenga más de un canal, hasta el punto en que dicho rio corta el lindero meridional de Nuevo México; continuará luego hácia al occidente por todo este lindero meridional (que corre al norte del pueblo llamado Paso) hasta su término por el lado del occidente; desde allí subirá la línea divisoria hácia al norte por el lindero occidental de Nuevo México, hasta donde éste lindero esté cortado por el primer brazo del Rio Gila (y si no está cortado por ningún brazo del Rio Gila, entónces hasta el punto del mismo lindero occidental más cercano al tal brazo, y de allí en una línea recta al mismo brazo;) continuará después por mitad de este brazo y del Rio Gila hasta su confluencia con el Rio Colorado; y desde la confluencia de ambos rios la línea divisoria, cortando el Colorado, seguirá el límite que separa la Alta de la Baja California hasta el Mar Pacífico.

Los linderos meridional y occidental de Nuevo México, de que habla este artículo, son los que marcan en la carta titulada: "Mapa de los Estados Unidos de México según lo organizado y definido por las varias actas del congreso de dicha república, construido por las mejores autoridades. Edicion revisada que publicó en Nueva York en 1847, J. Disturnell;" de la cual se agrega un ejemplar al presente tratado, firmado y sellado por los plenipotenciarios infraescritos. Y para evitar toda dificultad al trazar sobre la tierra el límite que separa la Alta de la Baja California, queda convenido que dicho límite consistirá en una línea recta tirada desde la mitad del Rio Gila en el punto donde se une con el Colorado, hasta un punto en la costa del Mar Pacífico, distante una legua marina al sur del punto más meridional del puerto de San Diego, según éste puerto está dibujado en el plano que levantó el año de 1782 el segundo piloto de la armada Española Don Juan Pantoja, y se publicó en Madrid el de 1802, en el Atlas para el viaje de las goletas Sutil y Méxicana; del cual plano se agrega copia firmada y sellada por los plenipotenciarios respectivos.

Para consignar la línea divisoria con la precisión debida en mapas fehacientes, y para establecer sobre la tierra mojones que pongan a la vista los límites de ambas repúblicas, segun quedan descritos en el presente artículo, nombrará cada uno de los dos gobiernos un comisario y un agrimensor, que se juntarán antes del término de un año contando desde la fecha del canje de las ratificaciones de éste tratado, en el puerto de San Diego, y procederán a señalar y demarcar la expresada línea divisoria en todo su curso hasta la desembocadura del Rio Bravo del Norte. Llevarán diarios y levantarán planos de sus operaciones; y el resultado convenido por ellos se tendrá por parte de éste tratado, y tendrá la misma fuerza que si estuviése inserto en él; debiendo convenir amistosamente los dos gobiernos en el arreglo de cuanto necesiten estos individuos, y en la escolta respectiva que deban llevar, siempre que se crea necesario.

La línea divisoria que se establece por éste artículo será religiosamente respetada por cada una de las dos repúblicas, y ninguna variacion se hará jamás en ella, sino de expreso y libre consentimiento de ambas naciones, otorgado legalmente por el gobierno general de cada una de ellas, con arreglo a su propia constitucion.

ARTICULO VI

Los buques y ciudadanos de los Estados Unidos tendrán en todo tiempo un libre y no interrumpido tránsito por el Golfo de California y por el Rio Colorado, desde su confluencia con el Gila, para sus posesiones y desde sus posesiones sitas al norte de la línea divisoria que queda marcada en el artículo precedente; entendiéndose que éste tránsito se ha de hacer navegando por el Golfo de California y por el Rio Colorado, y no por tierra, sin expreso consentimiento del gobierno Mexicano.

Si por reconocimientos que se practíquen se comprobáre la posibilidad y conveniencia de construír un camino, canal, o ferrocarril, que en todo o en parte corra sobre el Rio Gila o sobre alguna de sus márgenes derecha o izquierda en la latitud de una legua marina de uno o de otro lado del rio, los gobiernos de ambas repúblicas se pondrán de acuerdo sobre su construccion a fine de que sirvan igualmente para el uso y provecho de ambos países.

ARTICULO VII

Como el Rio de Gila y la parte del Rio Bravo del Norte que corre bajo el lindero meridional de Nuevo México se dividen por mitad entre las dos repúblicas, según lo establecido en el artículo quinto, la navegacion en el Gila y en la parte que queda indicada del Bravo, será libre y común a los buques y ciudadanos de ambos países, sin que por alguno de ellos pueda hacerse (sin consentimiento del otro) ninguna obra que impida o interrumpa en todo o en parte el ejercicio de éste derecho, ni aún con motivo de favorecer nuevos métodos de navegacion. Tampoco se podrá cobrar (sino en el caso de desembarco en alguna de sus riberas) ningún impuesto o contribucion bajo ninguna denominacion o título a los buques, efectos, mercancías o personas que naveguen en dichos rios. Si para hacerlos o mantenerlos navegables fuere necesario o conveniente establecer alguna contribucion o impuesto, no podrá ésto hacerse sin el consentimiento do los dos gobiernos.

Las estipulaciones contenidas en el presente artículo dejan ilesos los derechos territoriales de una y otra república dentro de los límites que les quedan marcados.

ARTICULO VIII

Los Mexicanos establecidos hoy en territorios pertenecientes antes a México, y que quedan para lo futuro dentro de los límites señalados por el presente tratado a los Estados Unidos, podrán permanecer en donde ahora habitan, o trasladarse en cualquier tiempo a la República Mexicana, conservando en los indicados territorios los bienes que poseen, o enagenándolos y pasando su valor a donde les convenga, sin que por ésta pueda exigirseles ningún género de contribucion, graváman o impuesto.

Los que prefieran permanecer en los indicados territorios, podrán conservar el título y derechos de ciudadanos Mexicanos, o adquirir el título y derechos de ciudadanos de los Estados Unidos. Más la eleccion entre una y otra ciudadanía deberán hacerla dentro de un año contado desde la fecha del canje de las ratificaciones de éste tratado. Y los que permanecieren en los indicados territorios después de transcurrido el año, sin haber declarado su intencion de retener el carácter de Mexicanos, se considerará que han elegido ser ciudadanos de los Estados Unidos.

Las propiedades de todo género existentes en los expresados territorios, y que pertenecen ahora a Mexicanos no establecidos en ellos, serán respetadas inviolablemente. Sus actuales dueños, los herederos de éstos, y los Mexicanos que en lo venidero pueden adquirir por contrato las indicadas propiedades, disfrutarán respecto de ellas tan amplia garantía, como si perteneciesen a ciudadanos de los Estados Unidos.

ARTICULO IX

Los Mexicanos que en los territorios antedichos no conserven el carácter de ciudadanos de la República Mexicana según lo estipulado en el artículo precedente, serán incorporados en la union de los Estados Unidos, y se admitirán en tiempo oportuno (a juicio del congreso de los Estados Unidos) al goce de todos los derechos de ciudadanos de los Estados Unidos conforme a los principios de la constitucion, y entretanto serán mantenidos y protegidos en el goce de su libertad y propiedad, y asegurados en el libre ejercicio de su religión sin restriccion alguna.

ARTICULO X

(Suprimido)

ARTICULO XI

En atencion a que una gran parte de los territorios que por el presente tratado van a quedar para lo futuro dentro de los límites de los Estados Unidos, se haya actualmente ocupado para tríbus salvajes, que han de estar en adelante bajo la exclusiva autoridad del gobierno de los Estados Unidos, y cuyas incursiones sobre los distritos Mexicanos serian en extremo perjudiciales; está solamente convenido que el mismo gobierno de los Estados Unidos contendrá las indicadas incursiones por medio de la fuerza, simpre que así sea necesario: y cuando no pudiere prevenirlas, castigará y escarmentará a los invasores, exigiendoles además la debida reparacion; todo del mismo modo, y con la misma diligencia y energía con que obraría, si las incursiones se hubiesen meditado o ejecutado sobre territorios suyos o contra sus propios ciudadanos.

A ningún habitante de los Estados Unidos será licito, bajo ningún pretesto, comprar o adquirir cautivo alguno, Mexicano, o extranjero, residente en México, apresado por los Indios habitantes en territorio de cualquiera de las dos repúblicas, ni los caballos, mulas, ganados, o cualquiera otro género de cosas que hayan robado dentro del territorio Mexicano.

Y en caso de que cualquier persona o personas cautivadas por los Indios dentro del territorio Mexicano sean llevadas al territorio de los Estados Unidos, el gobierno de dichos Estados Unidos se compromete y liga de la manera más solemne, en cuanto le sea posible, a rescatarlas, y restituirlas a su país, o entregarlas al agente o representante del gobierno Méxicano; haciendo todo ésto, tan luego como sepa que los dichos cautivos se hallan dentro de su territorio, y empleando al efecto el leal ejercicio de su influencia y poder. Las autoridades Mexicanas darán a los Estados Unidos, según sea practicable, una noticia de tales cautivos; y el agente Mexicano pagará los gastos erogados en el mantenimiento y remisión de los que se rescaten, los cuales entretanto serán tratados con la mayor hospitalidad por las autoridades Americanas del lugar en que se encuentren. Más si el gobierno de los Estados Unidos ántes de recibir aviso de México, tuviere noticia por cualquiera otro conducto de existir en su territorio cautivos Mexicanos, procederá desde luego a verificar su rescate y entrega al agente Mexicano, según queda convenido.

Con el objeto de dar a éstas estipulaciones la mayor fuerza posible, afianzar al mismo tiempo la seguridad y las reparaciones que exige el verdadero espíritu e intencion con que se han ajustado, el gobierno de los Estados Unidos dictará sin inútiles dilaciones, ahora y en lo de adelante, las leyes que requiera la naturaleza del asunto, y vigilará siempre sobre su ejecucion. Finalmente, el gobierno de los mismos Estados Unidos tendrá muy presente la santidad de ésta obligacion siempre que tenga que desalojar a los Indios de cualquier punto de los indicados territorios, o en él a ciudadanos suyos, y cuidará muy especialmente de que no se ponga a los Indios que habitaban ántes aquel punto, en necesidad de buscar nuevos hogares por medio de las incursiones sobre los distritos Mexicanos, que el gobierno de los Estados Unidos se ha comprometido solemnemente reprimir.

ARTICULO XII

En consideracion a la extensión que adquieren los límites de los Estados Unidos, según quedan descritos en el artículo quinto del presente tratado, el gobierno de los mismos Estados Unidos se compromete a pagar al de la Republican Mexicana la suma de quince millones de pesos.

Inmediatamente después que éste tratado haya sido ratificado por el gobierno de la República Mexicana, se entregará al mismo gobierno por el de los Estados Unidos, en la Ciudad de México, y en moneda de plata u oro de cuño Mexicano, la suma de tres millones de pesos. Los doce millones de pesos restantes se pagarán en México, en moneda de plata u oro del cuño Mexicano, en abonos de tres millones de pesos cada año, con un rédito de seis por ciento anual; éste rédito comienza a correr para toda la suma de los doce millones el día de la ratificacion del presente tratado por el gobierno Mexicano, y con cada abono anual de capital se pagará rédito que corresponda a la suma abonada. Los plazos para los abonos de capital corren desde el mismo día que empiezan a causarse los réditos.

ARTICULO XIII

Se obliga además el gobierno de los Estados Unidos a tomar sobre sí, y satisfacer cumplidamente a los reclamantes, todas las cantidades que hasta aquí se les deben y cuantas se venzan en adelante por razón de las reclamaciones ya liquidadas y sentenciadas contra la República Mexicana conforme a los convenios ajustados entre ambas repúblicas el 11 de Abril, 1839, y el 30 de Enero, 1843; de manera que la República Mexicana nada absolutamente tendrá que lastar en lo venidero, por razón de los indicados reclamos.

ARTICULO XIV

Tambien exoneran los Estados Unidos a la República Mexicana de todas las reclamaciones de ciudadanos de los Estados Unidos no decididas aún contra el gobierno Mexicano, y que puedan haberse originado ántes de la fecha de la firma del presente tratado; ésta exoneracion es definitiva y perpétua, bien sea que las dichas reclamaciones se admitan, bien sea que se desechen, por el tribunal de comisarios de que habla el artículo siguiente, y cualquiera que pueda ser el monto total de las que quedan admitidas.

ARTICULO XV

Los Estados Unidos, exonerando a México de toda responsabilidad por las reclamaciones de sus ciudadanos mencionadas en el artículo precedente, y considerandolas completamente canceladas para siempre, sea cual fuere su monto, toman a su cargo satisfacerlas hasta una cantidad que no exceda de tres millones doscientos cincuenta mil pesos. Para fijar el monto y validéz de éstas reclamaciones, se establecerá por el gobierno de los Estados Unidos un tribunal de comisarios, cuyos fallos serán definitivos y concluyentes: *Con tal:* Que al decidir sobre la validéz de dichas reclamaciones, el tribunal se haya guiado y gobernado por los principios y reglas de decisión establecidos en los artículos primero y quinto de la convencion, no ratificada, que se ajustó en la ciudad de México el veinte de Noviembre de mil ochocientos cuarenta y tres; y en ningún caso se dará fallo en favor de ninguna reclamacion que no esté comprendida en las reglas y principios indicados.

Si en juicio de dicho tribunal de comisarios, o en el de los reclamantes, se necesitare para la justa decisión de cualquier reclamacion algunos libros, papeles de archivo o documentos que posea el gobierno Mexicano, o que estén en su poder; los comisarios, o reclamantes por conducto de ellos, los pedirán por escrito (dentro del plazo que designe el congreso) dirigiéndose al ministro Mexicano de relaciones exteriores, a quien transmitirá las peticiones de ésta clase el secretario de estado de los Estados Unidos; y el gobierno Mexicano se compromete a entregar a la mayor brevedad posible, después de recibida cada demanda, los libros, papeles de archivo o documentos, así especificados, que posea o estén en su poder, o copias o extractos auténticos de los mismos, con el objeto de que sean transmitidos al secretario de estado, quien los pasará inmediatamente al expresado tribunal de comisarios. Y no se hará peticion alguna de los enunciados libros, papeles o documentos, por o instancia de ningún reclamante, sin que ántes se haya aseverado bajo juramento o con afirmacion solemne la verdad de los hechos que con ellos se pretende probar.

ARTICULO XVI

Cada una de las dos repúblicas se reserva la completa facultad de fortificar todos los puntos que para su seguridad estime convenientes en su propio territorio.

ARTICULO XVII

El tratado de amistad, comercio y navegacion, concluido en la Ciudad de México el 5 de Abril, del año del Señor 1831, entre la República Mexicana y los Estados Unidos de América, exceptuándose el artículo adicional y cuanto pueda hacer en sus estipulaciones incompatibles con alguna de las contenidas en el presente tratado, queda restablecido por el período de ocho años desde el día del canje de las ratificaciones del mismo presente tratado, con igual fuerza y virtud que si estuviese inserto en él; debiendo entenderse que cada una de las partes contratantes se reserva el derecho de poner término al dicho tratado de comercio y navegacion en cualquier tiempo luego que haya expirado el período de los ocho años, comunicando su intencion a la otra parte con un año de anticipacion.

ARTICULO XVIII

No se exigirán derechos ni gavámen de ninguna clase a los artículos todos que lleguen para las tropas de los Estados Unidos a los puertos Mexicanos ocupados por ellas, ántes de la evacuacion final de los mismos puertos, y después de la devolucion a México de las aduanas situadas en ellos. El gobierno de los Estados Unidos se compromete a la vez, y sobre ésto empeña su fé, a establecer y mantener con vigilancia cuantas guardias sean posibles para asegurar las rentas de México, precaviendo la importacion, a la sombra de ésta estipulacion, de cualesquiera artículos que realmente no sean necesarios, o que excedan en cualidad y cantidad de los que se necesiten para el uso y consumo de las fuerzas de los Estados Unidos mientras ellas permanezcan en México. A éste efecto, todos los oficiales y agentes de los Estados Unidos tendrán obligacion de denunciar a las autoridades Mexicanas en los mismos puertos, cualquier conato de fraudulento abuso de esta estipulacion que pudieran conocer o tuvieren motivo de sospechar; así como de impartir a las mismas autoridades todo el auxilio que pudieren con éste objeto; y cualquier conato de ésta clase, que fuere legalmente probado, y declarado por sentencia de tribunal competente, será castigado con el comiso de la cosa que se haya intentado introducir fraudulentamente.

ARTICULO XIX

Respecto de los efectos, mercancías y propiedades importados en los puertos Mexicanos durante el tiempo que han estado ocupados por las fuerzas de los Estados Unidos, sea por ciudadanos de cualquiera de las dos repúblicas, sea por ciudadanos o súbditos de alguna nacion neutral, se observarán las reglas siguientes:

Primera. Los dichos efectos, mercancías y propiedades siempre que se hayan importado ántes de la devolucion de las aduanas a las autoridades Mexicanas conforme a lo estipulado en el artículo tercero de éste tratado, quedarán libres de la pena de comiso; aún cuando sean de los prohibidos en el arancél Mexicano.

Segunda. La misma exencion gozarán los efectos, mercancías y propiedades que lleguen a los puertos Mexicanos, después de la devolucion a México de las aduanas marítimas, y ántes de que expiren los sesenta días que van a fijarse en el artículo siguiente para que empieze a regir el arancél Mexicano en los puertos; debiendo al tiempo de su importacion sujetarse los tales efectos, mercancías y propiedades, en cuanto al pago de derechos, a lo que en el indicado siguiente artículo se establece.

Tercera. Los efectos, mercancías y propiedades designados en las dos reglas anteriores quedarán exentos de todo derecho, alcabala o impuesto, sea bajo el título de internacion, sea bajo cualquiera otro, mientras permanezcan en los puntos donde se hayan importado, y a su salida para el interior; y en los mismos puntos no podrá jamás exigirse impuesto alguno sobre su venta.

Cuarta. Los efectos, mercancías y propiedades designados en las reglas primera y segunda que hayan sido internados a cualquier lugar ocupado por fuerzas de los Estados Unidos, quedarán exentos de todo derecho sobre su venta o consumo, y de todo impuesto o contribucion bajo cualquier título o denominacion, mientras permanezcan en el mismo lugar.

Quinta. Más si algunos efectos, mercancías o propiedades de los designados en las reglas primera y segunda se trasladaren a algún lugar no ocupado a la sazón por las fuerzas de los Estados Unidos; al introducirse a tal lugar, o al venderse o consumirse en él, quedarán sujetos a los mismos derechos que bajo las leyes Mexicanas deberían pagar en tales casos si se hubieran importado en tiempo de paz por las aduanas marítimas, y hubiesen pagado en ellas los derechos que establece el arancél Mexicano.

Sexta. Los dueños de efectos, mercancías y propiedades designadas en las reglas primera y segunda, y existentes en algún puerto de México, tienen derecho de reembarcarlos, sin que pueda exigirseles ninguna clase de impuesto, alcabala o contribucion.

Respecto de los metales y de toda otra propiedad exportados por cualquier puerto Mexicano durante su ocupacion por las fuerzas Americanas, y ántes de la devolucion de su aduana al gobierno Mexicano, no se exigirá a ninguna persona por las autoridades de México, ya dependan del gobierno general, ya de algún estado que pague algún impuesto, alcabala, o derecho por la indicada exportacion, ni sobre ella podrá exigirsele por las dichas autoridades cuenta alguna.

ARTICULO XX

Por consideracion a los intereses del comercio de todas las naciones, queda convenido que si pasaren ménos de sesenta días desde la fecha de la firma de éste tratado hasta que se haga la devolucion de las aduanas marítimas, según lo estipulado en el artículo tercero; todos los efectos, mercancías, y propiedades que lleguen a los puertos Mexicanos desde el día en que se verifique la devolucion de las dichas aduanas hasta que se completen sesenta días contados desde la fecha de la firma del presente tratado, se admitirán no pagando otros derechos que los establecidos en la tarifa que esté vigente en las expresadas aduanas al tiempo de su devolucion, y se extenderán a dichos efectos, mercancías, y propiedades las mismas reglas establecidas en el artículo anterior.

ARTICULO XXI

Si desgraciadamente en el tiempo futuro se suscitare algún punto de desacuerdo entre los gobiernos de las dos repúblicas, bien sea sobre la inteligencia de alguna estipulacion de éste tratado, bien sobre cualquiera otra materia de las relaciones políticas o comerciales de las dos naciones, los mismos gobiernos, a nombre de ellas, se comprometen a procurar de la manera más sincéra y empeñosa allanar las diferencias que se presenten y conservar el estado de paz y amistad en que ahora se ponen los dos países, usando al efecto de representaciones mutuas y de negociaciones pacíficas. Y si por estos medios no se lograre todavia ponerse de acuerdo, no por eso se apelarán represalia, agresión ni hostilidad de ningún género de una república contra otra, hasta que el gobierno de la que se crea agraviada haya considerado maduramente y en espiritu de paz y buena vecindad, si no sería mejor que la diferencia se terminará por una arbitracion de comisarios nombrados por ambas partes, o de una nacion amiga. Y si tal medio fuere propuesto por cualquiera de las dos partes, la otra accederá a él, a no ser que lo juzgue absolutamente incompatible con la naturaleza o circunstancias del caso.

ARTICULO XXII

Si (lo que no es de esperarse, y Dios no permita) desgraciadamente se suscitare guerra entre las dos repúblicas, éstas para el caso de tal calamidad se comprometen ahora solemnemente, ante si mismas y ante el mundo, a observar las reglas siguientes de una manera absoluta si la naturaleza del objeto a que se contraen lo permite; y tan estrictamente como sea dable en todos los casos en que la absoluta observancia de ellas fuere imposible.

Primero. Los comerciantes de cada una de las dos repúblicas que a la sazon residan en territorio de la otra, podrán permanecer doce meses los que residan en el interior, y seis meses los que residan en los puertos, para recoger sus deudas y arreglar sus negocios, durante estos plazos disfrutarán la misma proteccion y estarán sobre el mismo pié en todos respectos que los ciudadanos o súbditos de las naciones más amigas; y al expirar el término, o ántes de él, tendrán completa libertad para salir y llevar todos sus efectos sin molestia o embarazo, sujetándose en este particular a las mismas leyes a que estén sujetos, y deban arreglarse los ciudadanos o súbditos de las naciones más amigas. Cuando los ejércitos de una de las dos naciones entren en territorios de la otra, las mujeres y niños, los eclesiásticos, los estudiantes de cualquiera facultad, los labradores, comerciantes, artesanos, manufactureros, y pescadores que estén desarmados y residan en ciudades, pueblos o lugares no fortificados, y en general todas las personas cuya ocupacion sirva para la común subsistencia y beneficio del género humano, podrán continuar en sus ejercicios, sin que sus personas sean molestadas. No serán incendiadas sus casas o bienes, o destruidos de otra manera; ni serán tomados sus ganados, ni devastados sus campos por la fuerza armada en cuyo poder puedan venir a caer por los acontecimientos de la guerra; pero si hubiere necesidad de tomarles alguna cosa para el uso de la misma fuerza armada, se le pagará lo tomado a un precio justo. Todas las iglesias, hospitales, escuelas, colegios librerías y demás establecimientos de caridad y beneficencia serán respetados; y todas las personas que dependan de los mismos serán protegidas en el desempeño de sus deberes y en la continuacion de sus profesiones.

Segunda. Para aliviar la suerte de los prisioneros de guerra se evitarán cuidadosamente las prácticas de enviarlos a distritos distantes inclemes mal sanos, o de aglomerarlos en lugares estrechos y enfermizos. No se confinarán en calabozos, prisiones ni pontones; no se les aherrojar, ni se les atará, ni se les impedirá de ningún otro modo el uso de sus miembros. Los oficiales quedarán en libertad bajo su palabra de honor, dentro de distritos convenientes y tendrán alojamientos cómodos; y los soldados razos se colocarán en acantonamientos bastante despejados y extensos para la ventilacion y el ejercicio, y se alojarán en cuarteles tan amplios y cómodos como los que use para sus propias tropas la parte que los tenga en su poder. Pero si algún oficial faltare a su palabra, saliendo del distrito que se le ha señalado; o algún otro prisionero se fugare de los límites de su acantonamiento después que éstos se les hayan fijado, tal oficial o prisionero perderá el beneficio del presente artículo por lo que mira a su libertad bajo su palabra o en acantonamiento; y si algún oficial faltando así a su palabra, o algún soldado razo saliendo de los límites que se le han asignado, fuere encontrado después con armas en la mano ántes de ser debidamente canjeado, tal persona en ésta actitud ofensiva será tratada conforme a las leyes comúnes de la guerra. A los oficiales se proveerá diariamente por la parte en cuyo poder estén, de tantas raciones compuestas de los mismos artículos como las que gozan en especie o en equivalente los oficiales de la misma graduacion en su propio ejército, a todos los demás prisioneros se proveerá diariamente de una racion semejante a la que se ministra al soldado razo en su propio servicio, el valor de todas éstas suministraciones se pagará por la otra parte al concluirse la guerra, o en los períodos que se convengan entre sus respectivos comandantes, precediendo una mutua liquidacion de las cuentas que se lleven del mantenimiento de prisioneros, y tales cuentas no se mezclarán ni compensarán con otras, ni el saldo que resulte de ellas, se rehusará bajo pretexto de compensacion o represalia por cualquiera causa, real o figurada. Cada una de las partes podrá mantener un comisario de prisioneros nombrado por ella misma en cada acantonamiento de los prisioneros que estén en poder de la otra parte, éste comisario visitará a los prisioneros siempre que quiera, tendrá facultad de recibir, libres de todo derecho o impuesto, y de distribuir todos los auxilios que puedan enviarles sus amigos, y podrá libremente transmitir sus partes en cartas abiertas a la autoridad por la cual está empleado.

Y si declara, que ni el pretexto de que la guerra destruye los tratados, ni otro alguno, sea el que fuere, se considerará que anula, o suspende el pacto solemne contenido en éste artículo. Por el contrario, el estado de guerra es cabalmente el que se ha tenido presente al ajustarlo, y durante el cual sus estipulaciones se han de observar tan santamente como las obligaciones más reconocidas de la ley natural o de gentes.

ARTICULO XXIII

Este tratado será ratificado por el presidente de la República Mexicana, prévia la aprobacion de su congreso general, y por el presidente de los Estados Unidos de América, con el consejo y consentimiento del senado, y las ratificaciones se conjearán en la Ciudad de Washington, o donde estuviere el gobierno Mexicano, a los cuatro meses de la fecha de la firma del mismo tratado, o ántes si fuere posible.

En fé de lo cual, nosotros los respectivos plenipotenciarios, hemos firmado y sellado por quintuplicado, éste tratado de paz, amistad, límites y arreglo definitivo, en la Ciudad de Guadalupe Hidalgo, el día dos de Febrero, del año de nuestro Señor, mil ochocientos cuarenta y ocho.

BERNARDO COUTO,
MIG'L ATRISTAIN,
LUIS G. CUEVAS,
N.P. TRIST.

7

Organic Act Establishing the Territory of New Mexico, 1850

After the Taos rebellion and the death of Governor Bent in 1847, New Mexico came under military government. New Mexicans objected, but hopes for statehood or for territorial status were delayed by national political issues, particularly the question of slavery, which had been reopened by the Mexican War. The claim of Texas to the Rio Grande boundary also complicated the issue. Decisions regarding the status of New Mexico were made in Washington, and the Compromise of 1850 provided for a regular territorial government for New Mexico and established the Texas boundary within two miles of the present border.

ORGANIC ACT ESTABLISHING THE TERRITORY OF NEW MEXICO

(September 9, 1850)

Section 1. The following propositions shall be, and the same hereby are, offered to the state of Texas, which, when agreed to by the said state, in an act passed by the general assembly, shall be binding and obligatory upon the United States, and upon the said state of Texas: Provided, The said agreement by the said general assembly shall be given on or before the first day of December, eighteen hundred and fifty:

First. The state of Texas will agree that her boundary on the north shall commence at the point at which the meridian of one hundred degrees west from Greenwich is intersected by the parallel of thirty-six degrees thirty minutes north latitude, and shall run from said point due west to the meridian of one hundred and three degrees west from Greenwich; thence her boundary shall run due south to the thirty-second degree of north latitude; thence on the said parallel of thirty-two degrees of north latitude to the Rio Bravo del Norte, and thence with the channel of said river to the Gulf of Mexico.

Second. The state of Texas cedes to the United States all her claim to territory exterior to the limits and boundaries which she agrees to establish by the first article of this agreement.

Third. The state of Texas relinquishes all claim upon the United States for liability of the debts of Texas, and for compensation or indemnity for the surrender to the United States of her ships, forts, arsenals, custom-houses, custom-house revenue, arms and munitions of war, and public buildings with their sites, which became the property of the United States at the time of the annexation.

Fourth. The United States, in consideration of said establishment of boundaries, cession of claim to territory, and relinquishment of claims, will pay to the state of Texas the sum of ten millions of dollars in a stock bearing five per cent interest, and redeemable at the end of fourteen years, the interest payable half-yearly at the treasury of the United States.

Fifth. Immediately after the President of the United States shall have been furnished with an authentic copy of the act of the general assembly of Texas accepting these propositions, he shall cause the stock to be issued in favor of the state of Texas, as provided for in the fourth article of this agreement: Provided, also, That no more than five millions of said stock shall be issued until the creditors of the state holding bonds and other certificates of stock of Texas for which duties on imports were specially pledged, shall first file at the treasury of the United States releases of all claim against the United States for or on account of said bonds or certificates in such form as shall be prescribed by the secretary of the treasury and approved by the President of the United States: Provided, That nothing herein contained shall be construed to impair or qualify anything contained in the third article of the second section of the "joint resolution for annexing Texas to the United States," approved March first, eighteen hundred and forty-five, either as regards the number of states that may hereafter be formed out of the state of Texas, or otherwise.

Sec. 2. All that portion of the territory of the United States bounded as follows: Beginning at a point in the Colorado River where the boundary line with the Republic of Mexico crosses the same; thence eastwardly with the said boundary line to the Rio Grande; thence following the main channel of said river to the parallel of the thirty-second degree of north latitude; thence east with said degree to its intersection with the one hundred and third degree of longitude west of Greenwich; thence north with said degree of longitude to the parallel of thirty-eighth degree of north latitude; thence west with said parallel to the summit of the Sierra Madre; thence south with the crest of said mountains to the thirty-seventh parallel of north latitude; thence west with said parallel to its intersection with the boundary line of the state of California; thence with said boundary line to the place of beginning—is hereby, erected into a temporary government, by the name of the Territory of New Mexico: Provided, That nothing in this act contained shall be construed to inhibit the government of the United States from dividing said territory into two or more territories, in such manner and at such times as congress shall deem convenient and proper, or from attaching any portion thereof to any other territory or state: And provided, further, That, when admitted as a state, the said territory, or any portion of the same, shall be received into the Union, with or without slavery, as their Constitution may prescribe at the time of their admission.

Sec. 3. The executive power and authority in and over said Territory of New Mexico shall be vested in a governor, who shall hold his office for four years, and until his successor shall be appointed and qualified, unless sooner removed by the President of the United States. The governor shall reside within said territory, shall be commander-in-chief of the militia thereof, shall perform the duties and receive the emoluments of superintendent of Indian affairs, and shall approve all laws passed by the legislative assembly before they shall take effect; he may grant pardons for offenses against the laws of said territory, and reprieves for offenses against the laws of the United States, until the decision of the President can be made known thereon; he shall commission all officers who shall be appointed to office under the laws of the said territory, and shall take care that the laws be faithfully executed.

Sec. 4. There shall be a secretary of said territory, who shall reside therein, and hold his office for four years, unless sooner removed by the President of the United States; he shall record and preserve all the laws and proceedings of the legislative assembly hereinafter constituted, and all the acts and proceedings of the governor in his executive department; he shall transmit one copy of the laws and one copy of the executive proceedings, on or before the first day of December in each year, to the President of the United States, and, at the same time, two copies of the laws to the speaker of the house of representatives and the president of the senate, for the use of congress. And, in case of the death, removal, resignation, or other necessary absence of the governor from the territory, the secretary shall have, and he is hereby authorized and required to execute and perform all the powers and duties of the governor during such vacancy or necessary absence, or until another governor shall be duly appointed to fill such vacancy.

Sec. 5. The legislative power and authority of said territory shall be vested in the governor and a legislative assembly. The legislative assembly shall consist of a council and house of representatives. The council shall consist of thirteen members, having the qualifications of voters as hereinafter prescribed, whose term of service shall continue two years. The house of representatives shall consist of twenty-six members, possessing the same qualifications as prescribed for members of the council, and whose term of service shall continue one year. An apportionment shall be made, as nearly equal as practicable, among the several counties or districts, for the election of the council and house of representatives, giving to each section of the territory representation in the ratio of its population, (Indians excepted,) as nearly as may be. And the members of the council and of the house of representatives shall reside in, and be inhabitants of, the district for which they may be elected respectively. Previous to the first election, the governor shall cause a census or enumeration of the inhabitants of the several counties and districts of the territory to be taken, and the first election shall be held at such time and places, and be conducted in such manner, as the governor shall appoint and direct; and he shall, at the same time, declare the number of the members of the council and house of representatives to which each of the counties or districts shall be entitled under this act. The number of persons authorized to be elected having the highest number of votes in each of said council districts, for members of the council, shall be declared by the governor to be duly elected to the council; and the person or persons authorized to be elected having the greatest number of votes for the house of representatives, equal to the number to which each county or district shall be entitled, shall be declared by the governor to be duly elected members of the house of representatives: Provided, That in case of a tie between two or more persons voted for, the governor shall order a new election to supply the vacancy made by such tie. And the persons thus elected to the legislative assembly shall meet at such place and on such day as the governor shall appoint; but thereafter, the time, place, and manner of holding and conducting all elections by the people, and the apportioning the representation in the several counties or districts to the council and house of representatives according to the population, shall be prescribed by law, as well as the day of the commencement of the regular sessions of the legislative assembly: Provided, That no one session shall exceed the term of forty days.

Sec. 6. Every free white male inhabitant, above the age of twenty-one years, who shall have been a resident of said territory at the time of the passage of this act, shall be entitled to vote at the first election, and shall be eligible to any office within the said territory; but the qualifications of voters and of holding office, at all subsequent elections, shall be such as shall be prescribed by the legislative assembly: Provided, That the right of suffrage, and of holding office, shall be exercised only by citizens of the United States, including those recognized as citizens by the treaty with the Republic of Mexico, concluded February second, eighteen hundred and forty-eight.

Sec. 7. The legislative power of the territory shall extend to all rightful subjects of legislation, consistent with the Constitution of the United States and the provisions of this act; but no law shall be passed interfering with the primary disposal of the soil; no tax shall be imposed upon the property of the United States; nor shall the lands or other property of nonresidents be taxed higher than the lands or other property of residents. All the laws passed by the legislative assembly and governor shall be submitted to the Congress of the United States, and, if disapproved, shall be null and of no effect.

Sec. 8. All township, district, and county officers, not herein otherwise provided for, shall be appointed or elected, as the case may be, in such manner as shall be provided by the governor and legislative assembly of the Territory of New Mexico. The governor shall nominate, and, by and with the advice and consent of the legislative council, appoint, all officers not herein otherwise provided for; and in the first instance the governor alone may appoint all said officers, who shall hold their offices until the end of the first session of the legislative assembly, and shall lay off the necessary districts for members of the council and house of representatives, and all other officers.

Sec. 9. No member of the legislative assembly shall hold, or be appointed to, any office which shall have been created, or the salary or emoluments of which shall have been increased while he was a member, during the term for which he was elected, and for one year after the expiration of such term; and no person holding a commission or appointment under the United States, except postmasters, shall be a member of the legislative assembly, or shall hold any office under the government of said territory.

Sec. 10. The judicial power of said territory shall be vested in a Supreme Court, district courts, probate courts, and in justices of the peace. The Supreme Court shall consist of a chief justice and two associate justices, any two of whom shall constitute a quorum, and who shall hold a term at the seat of government of said territory annually, and they shall hold their offices during the period of four years. The said territory shall be divided into three judicial districts, and a district court shall be held in each of said districts by one of the justices of the Supreme Court, at such time and place as may be prescribed by law; and the said judges shall, after their appointments, respectively, reside in the districts which shall be assigned them. The jurisdiction of the several courts herein provided for, both appellate and original, and that of the probate courts and of justices of the peace, shall be as limited by law: Provided, That justices of the peace shall not have jurisdiction of any matter in controversy when the title or boundaries of land may be in dispute, or where the debt or sum claimed shall exceed one hundred dollars; and the said Supreme and district courts, respectively, shall possess chancery as well as common-law jurisdiction. Each district court, or the judge thereof, shall appoint its clerk, who shall also be the register in chancery, and shall keep his office at the place where the court may be held. Writs of error, bills of exception, and appeals, shall be allowed in all cases from the final decisions of said district courts to the Supreme Court, under such regulations as may be prescribed by law, but in no case removed to the Supreme Court shall trial by jury be allowed in said court. The Supreme Court, or the justices thereof, shall appoint its own clerk, and every clerk shall hold his office at the pleasure of the court for which he shall have been appointed. Writs of error and appeals from the final decisions of said Supreme Court shall be allowed, and may be taken to the Supreme Court of the United States, in the same manner and under the same regulations as from the circuit courts of the United States, where the value of the property or the amount in controversy, to be ascertained by the oath or affirmation of either party, or other competent witness, shall exceed one thousand dollars; except only that in all cases involving title to slaves, the said writs of error or appeals shall be allowed and decided by the said Supreme Court without regard to the value of the matter, property, or title in controversy; and except also that a writ of error or appeal shall also be allowed to the Supreme Court of the United States from the decision of the said Supreme Court created by this act, or of any judge thereof, or of the district courts created by this act, or of any judge thereof, upon any writ of habeas corpus involving the question of personal freedom; and each of the said district courts shall have and exercise the same jurisdiction in all cases arising under the Constitution and laws of the United States as is vested in the circuit and district courts of the United States; and the said Supreme and district courts of the said territory, and the respective judges thereof, shall and may grant writs of habeas corpus in all cases in which the same are grantable by the judges of the United States in the District of Columbia; and the first six days of every term of said courts, or so much thereof as shall be necessary, shall be appropriated to the trial of causes arising under the said Constitution and laws; and writs of error and appeals in all such cases shall be made to the Supreme Court of said territory, the same as in other cases. The said clerk shall receive in all such cases the same fees which the clerks of the district courts of Oregon territory now receive for similar services.

Sec. 11. There shall be appointed an attorney for said territory, who shall continue in office for four years, unless sooner removed by the President, and who shall receive the same fees and salary as the attorney of the United States for the present Territory of Oregon. There shall also be a marshal for the territory appointed, who shall hold his office for four years, unless sooner removed by the President, and who shall execute all processes issuing from the said courts when exercising their jurisdiction as circuit and district courts of the United States: he shall perform the duties, be subject to the same regulation and penalties, and be entitled to the same fees as the marshal of the district court of the United States for the present Territory of Oregon, and shall, in addition, be paid two hundred [dollars] annually as a compensation for extra services.

Sec. 12. The governor, secretary, chief justice and associate justices, attorney and marshal, shall be nominated, and, by and with the advice and consent of the senate, appointed by the President of the United States. The governor and secretary, to be appointed as aforesaid, shall, before they act as such, respectively take an oath or affirmation, before the district judge, or some justice of the peace in the limits of said territory, duly authorized to administer oaths and affirmations by the laws now in force therein, or before the chief justice or some associate justice of the Supreme Court of the United States, to support the Constitution of the United States, and faithfully to discharge the duties of their respective offices; which said oaths, when so taken, shall be certified by the person by whom the same shall have been taken, and such certificates shall be received and recorded by the said secretary among the executive proceedings; and the chief justice and associate justices, and all other civil officers in said territory, before they act as such, shall take a like oath or affirmation, before the said governor or secretary, or some judge or justice of the peace of the territory, who may be duly commissioned and qualified, which said oath or affirmation shall be certified and transmitted, by the person taking the same, to the secretary, to be by him recorded as aforesaid; and afterwards, the like oath or affirmation shall be taken, certified, and recorded, in such manner and form as may be prescribed by law. The governor shall receive an annual salary of fifteen hundred dollars as governor, and one thousand dollars as superintendent of Indian affairs. The chief justice and associate justices shall each receive an annual salary of eighteen hundred dollars. The secretary shall receive an annual salary of eighteen hundred dollars. The said salary shall be paid quarter-yearly, at the treasury of the United States. The members of the legislative assembly shall be entitled to receive three dollars each per day during their attendance at the sessions thereof, and three dollars each for every twenty miles' travel in going to and returning from the said sessions, estimated according to the nearest usually traveled route. There shall be appropriated annually the sum of one thousand dollars, to be expended by the governor, to defray the contingent expenses of the territory; there shall also be appropriated annually a sufficient sum to be expended by the secretary of the territory, and upon an estimate to be made by the secretary of the treasury of the United States, to defray the expenses of the legislative assembly, the printing of the laws, and other incidental expenses; and the secretary of the territory shall annually account to the secretary of the treasury of the United States for the manner in which the aforesaid sum shall have been expended.

Sec. 13. The legislative assembly of the Territory of New Mexico shall hold its first session at such time and place in said territory as the governor thereof shall appoint and direct; and at said first session, or as soon thereafter as they shall deem expedient, the governor and legislative assembly shall proceed to locate and establish the seat of government for said territory at such place as they may deem eligible; which place, however, shall thereafter be subject to be changed by the said governor and legislative assembly.

Sec. 14. A delegate to the house of representatives of the United States, to serve during each congress of the United States, may be elected by the voters qualified to elect members of the legislative assembly, who shall be entitled to the same rights and privileges as are exercised and enjoyed by the delegates from the several other territories of the United States to the said house of representatives. The first election shall be held at such time and places, and be conducted in such manner, as the governor shall appoint and direct; and at all subsequent elections, the times, places, and manner of holding the elections shall be prescribed by law. The person having the greatest number of votes shall be declared by the governor to be duly elected, and a certificate thereof shall be given accordingly: Provided, That such delegate shall receive no higher sum for mileage than is allowed by law to the delegate from Oregon.

Sec. 15. When the lands in said territory shall be surveyed under the direction of the government of the United States, preparatory to bringing the same into market, sections numbered sixteen and thirty-six in each township in said territory shall be, and the same are hereby, reserved for the purpose of being applied to schools in said territory, and in the states and territories hereafter to be erected out of the same.

Sec. 16. Temporarily and until otherwise provided by law, the governor of said territory may define the judicial districts of said territory, and assign the judges who may be appointed for said territory to the several districts, and also appoint the times and places for holding courts in the several counties or subdivisions in each of said judicial districts, by proclamation to be issued by him; but the legislative assembly, at their first or any subsequent session, may organize, alter, or modify such judicial districts, and assign the judges, and alter the times and places of holding the courts, as to them shall seem proper and convenient.

Sec. 17. The Constitution, and all laws of the United States which are not locally inapplicable, shall have the same force and effect within the said Territory of New Mexico as elsewhere within the United States.

Sec. 18. The provisions of this act are hereby suspended, until the boundary between the United States and the state of Texas shall be adjusted; and when such adjustment shall have been effected, the President of the United States shall issue his proclamation, declaring this act to be in full force and operation, and shall proceed to appoint the officers herein provided to be appointed in and for said territory.

Sec. 19. No citizen of the United States shall be deprived of his life, liberty, or property, in said territory, except by the judgment of his peers and the laws of the land.

Approved, Sept. 9, 1850.

8

President Fillmore's Proclamation Declaring the Organic Act in Force, 1850

The Compromise of 1850 was signed into law by President Millard Fillmore on December 13, 1850. Fillmore declared the Organic Act to be in force and quickly appointed James S. Calhoun, former Indian superintendent and an advocate of statehood, as the first regular territorial governor.

PROCLAMATION OF PRESIDENT DECLARING ORGANIC ACT IN FORCE.

By the President of the United States of America.

A PROCLAMATION.

Whereas by an act of the congress of the United States of the 9th of September, 1850, entitled "An Act proposing to the State of Texas the establishment of her northern and western boundaries, the relinquishment by the said State of all territory claimed by her exterior to said boundaries and of all her claims upon the United States, and to establish a Territorial government for New Mexico," it was provided that the following propositions should be, and the same were thereby, offered to the state of Texas, which, when agreed to by the said state in an act passed by the general assembly, should be binding and obligatory upon the United States and upon the said State of Texas, provided the said agreement by the general assembly should be given on or before the 1st day of December, 1850, namely:

"First. The state of Texas will agree that her boundary on the north shall commence at the point at which the meridian of 100 degrees west from Greenwich is intersected by the parallel of 36 degrees 30 minutes north latitude, and shall run from said point due west to the meridian of 103 degrees west from Greenwich; thence her boundary shall run due south to the thirty second degree of north latitude; thence on the parallel of thirty-two degrees of north latitude to the Rio Bravo del Norte, and thence with the channel of said river to the Gulf of Mexico.

"Second. The state of Texas cedes to the United States all her claims to the territory exterior to the limits and boundaries which she agrees to establish by the first article of this agreement.

"Third. The state of Texas relinquishes all claim upon the United States for liability of the debts of Texas and for compensation or indemnity for the surrender to the United States of her ships, forts, arsenals, custom-houses, custom-house revenue, arms and munitions of war, and public buildings with their sites, which became the property of the United States at the time of the annexation.

"Fourth. The United States, in consideration of said establishment of boundaries, cession of claim to territory, and relinquishment of claims, will pay to the state of Texas the sum of $10,000,000 in a stock bearing five per cent. interest, and redeemable at the end of fourteen years, the interest payable half-yearly at the treasury of the United States.

"Fifth. Immediately after the president of the United States shall have been furnished with an authentic copy of the act of the general assembly of Texas accepting these propositions, he shall cause the stock to be issued in favor of the state of Texas as provided for in the fourth article of this agreement: Provided, also, That no more than $5,000,000 of said stock shall be issued until the creditors of the state holding bonds and other certificates of stock of Texas for which duties on imports were specially pledged shall first file at the treasury of the United States release of all claim against the United States for or on account of said bonds or certificates in such form as shall be prescribed by the secretary of the treasury and approved by the president of the United States: Provided, That nothing herein contained shall be construed to impair or qualify anything contained in the third article of the second section of the "joint resolution for annexing Texas to the United States" approved March 1, 1845, either as regards the number of states that may hereafter be formed out of the state of Texas or otherwise:" and

Whereas it was further provided by the eighteenth section of the same act of congress "that the provisions of this act be, and they are hereby, suspended until the boundary between the United States and the state of Texas shall be adjusted, and when such adjustment shall have been effected the president of the United States shall issue his proclamation declaring this act to be in full force and operation;" and

Whereas the legislature of the state of Texas, by an act approved the 25th of November last, entitled "An act accepting the propositions made by the United States to the state of Texas in an act of the congress of the United States approved the 9th day of September, A.D. 1850, and entitled 'An act proposing to the state of Texas the establishment of her northern and western boundaries, the relinquishment by the said state of all territory claimed by her exterior to said boundaries and of all her claims upon the United States, and to establish a territorial government of New Mexico,' " of which act a copy authenticated under the seal of the state of Texas has been furnished to the president, enacts "that the state of Texas hereby agrees to and accepts said propositions, and it is hereby declared that the said state shall be bound by the terms thereof, according to their true import and meaning."

Now, therefore, I, Millard Fillmore, president of the United States of America, do hereby declare and proclaim that the said act of the congress of the United States of the 9th of September last, is in full force and operation.

Given under my hand, at the City of Washington, this 13th day of December, A.D. 1850, and the seventy-fifth of the Independence of these United States.

MILLARD FILLMORE.

By the President,
DANL. WEBSTER,
Secretary of State.

9

Gadsden Treaty, 1853

Following ratification of the Treaty of Guadalupe Hidalgo disputes occurred over the exact location of the international boundary and over control of Indians along the border. The gold rush to California and the desire to build a railroad across the West stimulated American interest in the region south of the Gila River. The offer by the United States to purchase this area was tendered to Antonio López de Santa Anna, who had returned to power in Mexico, and the Gadsden Purchase gave the United States the Mesilla Valley as well as the southern portion of the present state of Arizona.

THE GADSDEN TREATY

between the

UNITED STATES AND MEXICO

As Negotiated by James Gadsden, Envoy Extraordinary and Minister Plenipotentiary on the Part of the United States, Signed December 30, 1853

BY THE PRESIDENT OF
THE UNITED STATES OF AMERICA

A PROCLAMATION

WHEREAS, A treaty between the United States of America and the Mexican republic was concluded and signed at the City of Mexico on the thirtieth day of December, one thousand eight hundred and fifty-three; which treaty, as amended by the senate of the United States, and being in the English and Spanish languages, is word for word as follows:

IN THE NAME OF ALMIGHTY GOD:

The Republic of Mexico and the United States of America, desiring to remove every cause of disagreement which might interfere in any manner with the better friendship and intercourse between the two countries, and especially in respect to the true limits which should be established, when, notwithstanding what was covenanted in the treaty of Guadalupe Hidalgo in the year 1848, opposite interpretations have been urged, which might give occasion to questions of serious moment: to avoid these, and to strengthen and more firmly maintain the peace which happily prevails between the two republics, the President of the United States has, for this purpose, appointed James Gadsden, envoy extraordinary and minister plenipotentiary of the same, near the Mexican government, and the President of Mexico has appointed as plenipotentiary "ad hoc" his excellency Don Manual Diez de Bonilla, cavalier grand cross of the national and distinguished order of Guadalupe, and secretary of state, and of the office of foreign relations, and Don Jose Salazar Ylarregui and General Mariano Monterde as scientific commissioners, invested with full powers for this negotiation, who, having communicated their respective full powers, and finding them in due and proper form, have agreed upon the articles following:

ARTICLE I

The Mexican republic agrees to designate the following as her true limits with the United States for the future: retaining the same dividing line between the two Californias as already defined and established, according to the 5th article of the treaty of Guadalupe Hidalgo, the limits between the two republics shall be as follows: Beginning in the Gulf of Mexico, three leagues from land, opposite the mouth of the Rio Grande, as provided in the 5th article of the treaty of Guadalupe Hidalgo; thence, as defined in the said article, up the middle of that river to the point where the parallel of 31 deg. 47 min. north latitude crosses the same; thence due west one hundred miles; thence south to the parallel of 31 deg. 20 min. north latitude; thence along the said parallel of 31 deg. 20 min. to the 111th meridian of longitude west of Greenwich; thence in a straight line to a point on the Colorado River twenty English miles below the junction of the Gila and Colorado Rivers; thence up the middle of the said river Colorado until it intersects the present line between the United States and Mexico.

For the performance of this portion of the treaty, each of the two governments shall nominate one commissioner, to the end that, by common consent the two thus nominated, having met in the city of Paso del Norte, three months after the exchange of the ratifications of this treaty, may proceed to survey and mark out upon the land the dividing line stipulated by this article, where it shall not have already been surveyed and established by the mixed commission, according to the treaty of Guadalupe, keeping a journal and making proper plans of their operations. For this purpose, if they should judge it necessary, the contracting parties shall be at liberty each to unite to its respective commissioner, scientific or other assistants, such as astronomers and surveyors, whose concurrence shall not be considered necessary for the settlement and ratification of a true line of division between the two republics; that line shall be alone established upon which the commissioners may fix, their consent in this particular being considered decisive and an integral part of this treaty, without necessity of ulterior ratification or approval, and without room for interpretation of any kind by either of the parties contracting.

The dividing line thus established shall, in all time, be faithfully respected by the two governments, without any variation therein, unless of the express and free consent of the two, given in conformity to the principles of the law of nations, and in accordance with the Constitution of each country respectively.

In consequence, the stipulation in the 5th article of the treaty of Guadalupe upon the boundary line therein described is no longer of any force, wherein it may conflict with that here established, the said line being considered annulled and abolished wherever it may not coincide with the present, and in the same manner remaining in full force where in accordance with the same.

ARTICLE II

The government of Mexico hereby releases the United States from all liability on account of the obligations contained in the eleventh article of the treaty of Guadalupe Hidalgo; and the said article and the thirty-third article of the treaty of amity, commerce, and navigation between the United States of America and the united Mexican states concluded at Mexico, on the fifth day of April, 1831, are hereby abrogated.

ARTICLE III

In consideration of the foregoing stipulations, the government of the United States agrees to pay to the government of Mexico, in the city of New York, the sum of ten millions of dollars, of which seven millions shall be paid immediately upon the exchange of the ratifications of this treaty, and the remaining three millions as soon as the boundary line shall be surveyed, marked, and established.

ARTICLE IV

The provisions of the 6th and 7th articles of the treaty of Guadalupe Hidalgo having been rendered nugatory, for the most part, by the cession of territory granted in the first article of this treaty, the said articles are hereby abrogated and annulled, and the provisions as herein expressed substituted therefor. The vessels, and citizens of the United States shall, in all time, have free and uninterrupted passage through the Gulf of California, to and from their possessions situated north of the boundary line of the two countries. It being understood that this passage is to be by navigating the Gulf of California and the river Colorado, and not by land, without the express consent of the Mexican government; and precisely the same provisions, stipulations, and restrictions, in all respects, are hereby agreed upon and adopted, and shall be scrupulously observed and enforced by the two contracting governments in reference to the Rio Colorado, so far and for such distance as the middle of that river is made their common boundary line by the first article of this treaty.

The several provisions, stipulations, and restrictions contained in the 7th article of the treaty of Guadalupe Hidalgo shall remain in force only so far as regards the Rio Bravo del Norte, below the initial of the said boundary provided in the first article of this treaty; that is to say, below the intersection of the 31 deg. 47 min. 30 sec. parallel of latitude, with the boundary line established by the late treaty dividing said river from its mouth upwards, according to the fifth article of the treaty of Guadalupe.

ARTICLE V

All the provisions of the eighth and ninth, sixteenth and seventeenth articles of the treaty of Guadalupe Hidalgo, shall apply to the territory ceded by the Mexican republic in the first article of the present treaty, and to all the rights of persons and property, both civil and ecclesiastical, within the same, as fully and as effectually as if the said articles were herein again recited and set forth.

ARTICLE VI

No grants of land within the territory ceded by the first article of this treaty bearing date subsequent to the day—twenty-fifth of September—when the minister and subscriber to this treaty on the part of the United States, proposed to the government of Mexico to terminate the question of boundary, will be considered valid or be recognized by the United States, or will any grants made previously be respected or be considered as obligatory which have not been located and duly recorded in the archives of Mexico.

ARTICLE VII

Should there at any future period (which God forbid) occur any disagreement between the two nations which might lead to a rupture of their relations and reciprocal peace, they bind themselves in like manner to procure by every possible method the adjustment of every difference; and should they still in this manner not succeed, never will they proceed to a declaration of war, without having previously paid attention to what has been set forth in article twenty-one of the treaty of Guadalupe for similar cases; which article, as well as the twenty-second, is here reaffirmed.

ARTICLE VIII

The Mexican government having on the 5th of February, 1853, authorized the early construction of a plank and railroad across the Isthmus of Tehuantepec, and, to secure the stable benefits of said transit way to the persons and merchandise of the citizens of Mexico and the United States, it is stipulated that neither government will interpose any obstacle to the transit of persons and merchandise of both nations; and at no time shall higher charges be made on the transit of persons and property of citizens of the United States, than may be made on the persons and property of other foreign nations, nor shall any interest in said transit way, nor in the proceeds thereof, be transferred to any foreign government.

The United States, by its agents, shall have the right to transport across the isthmus, in closed bags, the mails of the United States not intended for distribution along the line of communication; also the effects of the United States government and its citizens, which may be intended for transit, and not for distribution on the isthmus, free of custom-house or other charges by the Mexican government. Neither passports nor letters of security will be required of persons crossing the isthmus and not remaining in the country.

When the construction of the railroad shall be completed, the Mexican government agrees to open a port of entry in addition to the port of Vera Cruz, at or near the terminus of said road on the Gulf of Mexico.

The two governments will enter into arrangements for the prompt transit of troops and munitions of the United States, which that government may have occasion to send from one part of its territory to another, lying on opposite sides of the continent.

The Mexican government having agreed to protect with its whole power the prosecution, preservation, and security of the work, the United States may extend its protection as it shall judge wise to it when it may feel sanctioned and warranted by the public or international law.

ARTICLE IX

This treaty shall be ratified, and the respective ratifications shall be exchanged at the city of Washington within the exact period of six months from the date of its signature, or sooner, if possible.

In testimony whereof, we, the plenipotentiaries of the contracting parties, have hereunto affixed our hands and seals at Mexico, the thirtieth (30) day of December, in the year of our Lord one thousand eight hundred and fifty-three, in the thirty-third year of the independence of the Mexican republic, and the seventy-eighth of that of the United States.

JAMES GADSDEN,
MANUAL DIEZ DE BONILLA,
JOSE SALAZAR YLARREGUI,
J. MARIANO MONTERDE,

And whereas the said treaty, as amended, has been duly ratified on both parts, and the respective ratifications of the same have this day been exchanged at Washington, by William L. Marcy, secretary of state of the United States, and Senor General Don Juan N. Almonte, envoy extraordinary and minister plenipotentiary of the Mexican republic, on the part of their respective governments:

Now, therefore, be it known that I, Franklin Pierce, President of the United States of America, have caused the said treaty to be made public, to the end that the same, and every clause and article thereof, may be observed and fulfilled with good faith by the United States and the citizens thereof.

In witness whereof I have hereunto set my hand and caused the seal of the United States to be affixed.

Done at the city of Washington, this thirtieth day of June, in the year of our Lord one thousand eight hundred and fifty-four, and of the independence of the United States the seventy-eighth.

FRANKLIN PIERCE.

By the President:
W.L. MARCY,
Secretary of State.

EL TRATADO DE GADSDEN

entre los

ESTADOS UNIDOS Y MEXICO

Segun Celebrado por James Gadsden, Enviado Extraordinario y Ministro Plenipotenciario por la parte de los Estados Unidos, Firmado Diciembre 30, 1853.

POR EL PRESIDENTE DE LOS ESTADOS UNIDOS DE AMERICA.

PROCLAMACION

POR CUANTO, un tratado entre los Estados Unidos de América y la República Mexicana, fué consumado y firmado en la Ciudad de México, el día treinta de Diciembre, mil ochocientos cincuenta y tres, cuyo tratado según enmendado por el senado de los Estados Unidos, y siendo en los idiomas Inglés y Español, es palabra por palabra como sigue:

EN EL NOMBRE DE DIOS TODOPODEROSO:

La República de México y los Estados Unidos de América, deseando remover toda causa de desacuerdo que pudiera influir en algún modo, en contra de la mejor amistad y correspondencia entre ambos países, y especialmente por lo respectivo a los verdaderos límites que deben fijarse, cuando no obstante, lo pactado en el tratado de Guadalupe Hidalgo, en el año de 1848, aún se han suscitado algunas interpretaciones encontradas que pudieran ser ocasión de cuestiones de grave trascendencia, para evitarlas, y afirmar y corroborar más la paz que felizmente reina entre ambas repúblicas, el presidente de México, ha nombrado a éste fin con el carácter de plenipotenciario *ad hoc* al Exmo. Sr. Don Manuel Diez de Bonilla, caballero gran cruz de la nacional y distinguida órden de Guadalupe, y Secretario de Estado, y del Despacho de Relaciones Exteriores, y a los Señores Don José Salazar Ylarreguí y General D. Mariano Monterde, como comisarios peritos investidos con plenos poderes para esta negociación, y el presidente de los Estados Unidos, a S.E. el Sr. Santiago Gadsden, Enviado Extraordinario y Ministro Plenipotenciario de los mismos Estados Unidos, cerca del gobierno Mexicano, quienes, habiéndose comunicado sus respectivos plenos poderes, y hallándolos en buena y debida forma, han convenido en los artículos siguientes:

ARTICULO I

La República Mexicana, conviene en señalar para lo sucesivo como verdaderos límites con los Estados Unidos, los siguientes: Subsistiendo la misma línea divisoria entre las dos Californias, tal cual está ya definida y marcada conforme al artículo quinto del tratado de Guadalupe Hidalgo, los límites entre las dos repúblicas, serán los que siguen: comenzando en el Golfo de México a tres leguas de distancia de la costa, frente a la desembocadura del Rio Grande, como se estipuló en el artículo quinto del tratado de Guadalupe Hidalgo, de allí, según se fija en dicho artículo, hasta la mitad de aquel rio al punto donde la paralela 31 grados, 47 minutos de latitud norte, atraviesa el mismo rio, de allí, cien millas en línea recta al oeste, de allí, al sur a la paralela de 31 grados, 20 minutos, de latitud norte, de allí, siguiendo la dicha paralela de 31 grados, 20 minutos, hasta el 111 del meridiano de longitud oeste de Greenwich, de allí, en línea recta a un punto en el Rio Colorado, veinte millas inglesas abajo de la unión de los Rios Gila y Colorado, de allí, por la mitad del dicho Rio Colorado hasta donde encuentra la actual línea divisoria entre los Estados Unidos y México.

Para la ejecucion de ésta parte del tratado, cada uno de los gobiernos nombrará un comisario para el fin que por común consentimiento, los dos así nombrados, habiéndose encontrado en la Ciudad del Paso del Norte, tres meses después del canje de las ratificaciones de éste tratado, puedan proceder a agrimensar y marcar sobre el terreno la línea divisoria estipulada por éste artículo, en lo que no estuviere ya reconocida y establecida por la comisión mixta según el tratado de Guadalupe, llevando al efecto diarios de sus procedimientos, y levantando los planos convenientes. A este efecto, si lo juzgaren necesario, las partes contratantes, podrán añadir a su respectivo comisario alguno o algunos auxiliarse, bien facultativos o no, como agrimensores, astrónomos, etc., pero sin que por esto su concurrencia se considere necesaria para la fijacion y ratificacion como verdadera línea divisoria entre ambas repúblicas, pues dicha línea solo será establecida por lo que convengan los comisarios, reputándose su conformidad en éste punto como decisiva y parte integrante de éste tratado, sin necesidad de ulterior ratificacion o aprobacion, y sin lugar a interpretacion de ningún género por cualquiera de las dos partes contratantes.

La línea divisoria establecida de éste modo, será en todo tiempo fielmente respetada por los dos gobiernos, sin permitirse ninguna variacion en ella, sino es de expreso y libre consentimiento de los dos, otorgado de conformidad con los principios del derecho de gentes, y con arreglo a la constitucion de cada país respectivamente. En consecuencia, lo estipulado en el artículo quinto del tratado de Guadalupe sobre la línea divisoria en él descrita, queda sin valor en lo que repugne con la establecida aquí, dándose por lo mismo por derogada y anulada dicha línea en la parte en que no es conforme con la presente, así como permanecerá en todo su vigor en la parte en que tuviere dicha conformidad con ella.

ARTICULO II

El gobierno de México por éste artículo, exime al de los Estados Unidos de las obligaciones del artículo once del tratado de Guadalupe Hidalgo, y dicho artículo, y el 33 del tratado de amistad, comercio y navegacion entre los Estados Unidos Mexicanos y los Estados Unidos de América, y concluido en México, el día 5 de Abril, de 1831, quedan por éste derogados.

ARTICULO III

En consideracion a las anteriores estipulaciones, el gobierno de los Estados Unidos conviene en pagar al gobierno de México, en la Ciudad de Nueva York, la suma de diez millones de pesos, de los cuales siete millones se pagarán luego que se verifique el canje de las ratificaciones de ese tratado, y los tres millones restantes tan pronto como se reconozca, marque, y fije la línea divisoria.

ARTICULO IV

Habiéndose hecho en su mayor parte nugatorias las estipulaciones de los artículos sexto y sétimo, del tratado de Guadalupe Hidalgo, por la cesión de territorios hecha en el artículo primero de éste tratado, aquellos dichos artículos, quedan por éste derogados y anulados, y las estipulaciones que a continuacion se expresan, substituidas en lugar de aquellas. Los buques y ciudadanos de los Estados Unidos tendrán en todo tiempo libre, y no interrumpido tránsito por el Golfo de California, para sus posesiones, y desde sus posesiones sitas al norte de la línea divisoria de los dos países, entendiéndose, que ese tránsito se ha de hacer navegando por el Golfo de California y por el Rio Colorado, y no por tierra, sin expreso consentimiento del gobierno Mexicano. Y precisamente, y bajo todos respectos, las mismas disposiciones, estipulaciones y restricciones quedan convenidas y adoptadas por éste artículo, y serán escrupulosamente observadas y hechas efectivas por los dos gobiernos contratantes, con referencia al Rio Colorado por tal distancia, y en tanto que la medianía de ese rio queda como su línea divisoria común, por el artículo primero de éste tratado. Las diversas disposiciones, estipulaciones y restricciones contenidas en el artículo sétimo del tratado de Guadalupe Hidalgo, solo permanecerán en vigor en lo relativo al Rio Bravo del Norte, abajo del punto inicial de dicho límite estipulado en el artículo primero de éste tratado, es decir, abajo de la interseccion del paralelo de 31 grados, 47 minutos, 30 segundos de latitud con la línea divisoria establecida por el reciente tratado que divide dicho rio desde su embocadura arriba, de conformidad con el artículo quinto del tratado de Guadalupe.

ARTICULO V

Todas las estipulaciones de los artículos, octavo, noveno, décimo sexto y décimo sétimo del tratado de Guadalupe Hidalgo, se aplicarán al territorio cedido por la República Mexicana en el artículo primero del presente tratado, y a todos los derechos de persona y bienes, tanto civiles como eclesiásticos, que se encuentren dentro de dicho territorio, tan plena y tan eficazmente como si dichos artículos de nuevo se insertaran e incluyeran a la letra en éste.

ARTICULO VI

No se considerarán válidas, ni se reconocerá por los Estados Unidos ningunas concesiones de tierra en el territorio, cedido por el artículo primero de éste tratado, de fecha subsecuente al día veinte y cinco de Setiembre, en que el ministro y signatario de éste tratado por parte de los Estados Unidos, propuso al gobierno de México dirimir la cuestión de límites, ni tampoco se respetarán, ni considerarán como obligatorias, ningunas concesiones hechas con anterioridad que no hayan sido inscritas y debidamente registradas en los archivos de México.

ARTICULO VII

Si en lo futuro, (que Dios no permita,) se suscitare algún desacuerdo entre las dos naciones, que pudiera llevarlas a un rompimiento de sus relaciones y paz recíproca, se comprometen así mismo a procurar por todos los medios posibles el allanamiento de cualquiera diferencia, y si aún de esta manera no se consiguiere, jamás se llegará a una declaracion de guerra sin haber observado previamente cuanto en el artículo veintiuno del tratado de Guadalupe, quedó establecido para semejantes casos, y cuyo artículo se dá por reafirmado en éste tratado, así como el veintidos.

ARTICULO VIII

Habiendo autorizado el gobierno Mexicano en 5 de Febrero, de 1853, la pronta construccion de un camino de madera y de un ferrocarril en el istmo de Tehuantepec, para asegurar de una manera estable los beneficios de dicha vía de comunicacion a las personas y mercancías de los ciudadanos de México y de los Estados Unidos, se estipula, que ninguno de los dos gobiernos, pondrá obstáculo alguno al tránsito de personas y mercancías de ambas naciones, y que en ningún tiempo se impondrán cargas por el tránsito de personas y propiedades de ciudadanos de los Estados Unidos, mayores que las que se impongan a las personas y propiedades de otras naciones extranjeras, y ningún interés en dicha vía de comunicacion, o en sus productos, se transferirá a un gobierno extranjero.

Los Estados Unidos tendrán derecho de transportar por el istmo, por medio de sus agentes y en balijas cerradas, los correos de los Estados Unidos que no han de distribuirse en la extensión de la línea de comunicacion, y tambien los efectos del gobierno de los Estados Unidos y sus ciudadanos, que solo vayan de transito, y no para distribuirse en el istmo, estarán libres, de los derechos de aduana, u otros impuestos por el gobierno Mexicano. No se exigirá a las personas que atraviesen el istmo, y no permanezcan en el país, pasaportes ni cartas de seguridad.

Cuando se concluya la construccion del ferrocarril, el gobierno Mexicano conviene en abrir un puerto de entrada, además del de Vera Cruz, en donde termina dicho ferrocarril en el Golfo de México, o cerca de ese punto.

Los dos gobiernos celebrarán un arreglo para el pronto tránsito de tropas y municiones de los Estados Unidos, que éste gobierno tenga ocasión de enviar de una parte de su territorio a otra, situadas en lados opuestos del continente.

Habiendo convenido el gobierno Mexicano en proteger con todo su poder la construccion, conservacion, y seguridad de la obra, los Estados Unidos de su parte, podrán impartirle su proteccion, siempre que fuere apoyado y arreglado al derecho de gentes o ley internacional.

ARTICULO IX

Este tratado será ratificado, y las ratificaciones respectivas canjeadas en la Ciudad de Washington, en el preciso término, de seis meses, o ántes si fuere posible, contado ese término desde su fecha.

En fé de lo cual, nosotros los plenipotenciarios de las partes contratantes lo hemos firmado y sellado, en México, el día treinta de Diciembre, del año de nuestro Señor, mil ochocientos cincuenta y tres, trigésimo tercero de la Independencia, de la República Mexicana, y septuagésimo octavo de los Estados Unidos.

JAMES GADSDEN,
MANUEL DIEZ DE BONILLA,
JOSE SALAZAR YLARREGUI.
J. MARIANO MONTERDE,

Y, por cuanto, el dicho tratado, según enmendado, ha sido debidamente ratificado por ambas partes, y las respectivas ratificaciones del mismo han sido hoy canjeadas en Washington, por William L. Marcy, Secretario de Estado de los Estados Unidos, y el Señor General Don Juan N. Almonte, Enviado Extraordinario y Ministro Plenipotenciario de la República Mexicana, por parte de sus respectivos gobiernos.

Por tanto, sabed que yo, Franklin Pierce, Presidente de los Estados Unidos de América, he causado, que dicho tratado se haga público con el fin de que el mismo, y cada cláusula y artículo en él contenido, sea observado y cumplido con buena fé por los Estados Unidos y sus ciudadanos.

En testimonio de lo cual he puesto mi mano y causado que el sello de los Estados Unidos se estampe a éste.

Dado en la Ciudad de Washington, hoy trienta de Junio, año de nuestro Señor, de mil ochocientos cincuenta y cuatro, y de la Independencia de los Estados Unidos, setenta y ocho.

FRANKLIN PIERCE.

Por el Presidente:
W.L. MARCY,
Secretario de Estado.

10

Governor Connelly's Proclamation on the Civil War, 1861

Following the outbreak of the Civil War, many of the high-ranking officers in the United States Army in New Mexico resigned their commissions and joined the Confederacy. In the summer of 1861 Colonel John R. Baylor led a Confederate invasion from El Paso. President Abraham Lincoln appointed Colonel E.R.S. Canby to command Union forces in New Mexico and selected Dr. Henry Connelly, a merchant and landowner from Peralta, as territorial governor. Connelly's proclamation was intended to arouse support for the Union cause.

GOVERNOR'S PROCLAMATION
September 9, 1861

WHEREAS this Territory is now invaded by an armed force from the State of Texas which has taken possession of two Forts within the limits of the Territory, has seized and appropriated to its own use other property of the General Government and has established military rule over the part already invaded; and:

WHEREAS, there is every reason to believe it is the intention of the said force to pursue its aggressions further and establish the same military rule over the balance of the Territory and subject us to the dominion and laws of the Government of Texas;

AND WHEREAS, By section 43 of an act of the Legislative Assembly approved January 6, 1852, it is provided that "in case of an insurrection, rebellion, or invasion, the Governor shall have power to organize and call out the militia for the service in such numbers, and form such districts as he may think proper:"

Now therefore I HENRY CONNELLY, Governor of the Territory of New Mexico, by the authority in me vested, do hereby issue this my proclamation ordering an immediate organization of the militia force in the different counties of this Territory and calling upon all officers, civil and military, to begin at once this organization. To effect this object the field officers provided for by the said militia law will be immediately appointed. The Adjutant General of the militia of the Territory is hereby ordered to carry this proclamation into immediate effect.

Citizens of New Mexico, your Territory has been invaded, the integrity of your soil has been attacked, the property of peaceful and industrious citizens has been destroyed or converted to the use of the invaders, and the enemy is already at your doors. You cannot, you must not, hesitate to take up arms in defense of your homes, firesides and families. Your manhood calls upon you to be on the alert and to be vigilant in the protection of the soil of your birth, where repose the sacred remains of your ancestors and which was left by them as a rich heritage to you, if you have the valor to defend it. I feel that I appeal not in vain to those who love the land of their fathers; a land that has been the scene of heroic acts, and deeds of noble daring in wars no more patriotic than that for which preparations are now being made. As your ancestors met the emergencies which presented themselves in reclaiming your country from the dominion of the savage and in preparing it for the abode of christianity and civilization, so must you now prove yourselves equal to the occasion and nerve your arms for the approaching conflict.

He whose heart beats with no patriotic impulse in times of danger, deserves not a *patria,* and should be treated as an enemy to his country. Of these, I trust there are few, if any, among us; but he that now falters, when every energy that exists in the patriotic heart should be brought into requisition for the purpose of repelling an invading foe will in future be pointed at with derision as an Arnold or as a Lynde.

Done at Santa Fe this 9th day of September in the year eighteen hundred and sixty one.

By the Governor,   HENRY CONNELLY.
M.A. OTERO,
Secretary of New Mexico.

11

Organic Act Separating Arizona from New Mexico, 1863

During the 1850s settlers in present-day Arizona appealed for separation from New Mexico, and Civil War secessionist sentiment there and in the Mesilla Valley led Colonel Baylor to create the Confederate Territory of Arizona in January 1862. The restoration of Union control by Colonel James Carleton caused renewed efforts to secure Union approval for a territory. Heavy lobbying resulted in the 1863 Organic Act, which passed with the support of New Mexico territorial delegate John S. Watts, and which established the western boundary of New Mexico.

An Act To Provide a Temporary Government for the Territory of Arizona and for Other Purposes

SECTION 1. *Be it enacted by the senate and the house of representatives of the United States of America in congress assembled* That all that part of the present Territory of New Mexico situate west of a line running due south from the point where the southwest corner of the Territory of Colorado joins the northern boundary of the Territory of New Mexico, to the southern boundary line of said Territory of New Mexico, be, and the same is hereby, erected into a temporary government, by the name of the Territory of Arizona: Provided, That nothing contained in the provisions of this act shall be construed to prohibit the Congress of the United States from dividing said Territory, or changing its boundaries, in such manner and at such time as it may deem proper: Provided, further, That said government shall be maintained and continued until such time as the people residing in said Territory shall, with the consent of Congress, form a State government, republican in form, as prescribed in the Constitution of the United States, and apply for and obtain admission into the Union as a State, on an equal footing with the original States.

SEC. 2. And be it further enacted, That the government hereby authorized shall consist of an executive, legislative, and judicial power. The executive power shall be vested in a Governor. The legislative power shall consist of a council of nine members and a house of representatives of eighteen. The judicial power shall be vested in a supreme court, to consist of three judges, and such inferior courts as the legislative council may by law prescribe; there shall also be a Secretary, a Marshal, a District Attorney, and a Surveyor general for said Territory, who, together with the governor and judges of the Supreme Court, shall be appointed by the President, by and with the advice and consent of the Senate, and the term of office for each, the manner of their appointment, and the powers, duties, and the compensation of the governor, legislative assembly, judges of the supreme court, secretary, marshal, district attorney, and surveyor general aforesaid, with their clerks, draughtsman, deputies, and sergeant-at-arms, shall be such as are conferred upon the same officers by the act organizing the territorial government of New Mexico, which subordinate officers shall be appointed in the same manner, and not exceed in number those created by said act, and acts amendatory thereto, together with all legislative enactments of the Territory of New Mexico not inconsistent with the provisions of this act are hereby extended to and continued in force in the said Territory of Arizona until repealed or amended by future legislation. Provided, That no salary shall be due or paid the officers created by this act until they have entered upon the duties of their respective offices within the said Territory.

SEC. 3. And be it further enacted. That there shall neither be slavery nor involuntary servitude in the said Territory, otherwise than in the punishment of crimes, whereof the parties shall have been duly convicted; and all acts and parts of acts, either of Congress or of the Territory of New Mexico, establishing, regulating, or in any way recognizing the relation of master and slave in said Territory are hereby repealed.

GALUSHA A. GROW
Speaker of the House of Representatives
SOLOMON FOOT
President of the Senate pro tempore.

Approved, February 24, 1863
ABRAHAM LINCOLN

12

Act of Congress Abolishing Peonage in New Mexico, 1867

Before the Civil War both debt peonage and Indian slavery existed in New Mexico, and during the Reconstruction era Congress enacted legislation to abolish peonage. Many New Mexicans ignored the law, and in 1868 Congress passed a joint resolution authorizing the army to free peons from bondage.

An Act to Abolish and Forever Prohibit the System of Peonage in the Territory of New Mexico and Other Parts of the United States.

39th Congress, 2d session

Be it enacted by the Senate and House of Representatives of the United States of America in Congress assembled, That the holding of any person to service or labor under the system known as peonage is hereby declared to be unlawful, and the same is hereby abolished and forever prohibited in the Territory of New Mexico, or in any other Territory or State of the United States; and all acts, laws, resolutions, orders, regulations, or usages of the Territory of New Mexico, or of any other Territory or State of the United States, which have heretofore established, maintained, or enforced, or by virtue of which any attempt shall hereafter be made to establish, maintain, or enforce, directly or indirectly, the voluntary or involuntary service or labor of any persons as peons, in liquidation of any debt or obligation, or otherwise, be, and the same are hereby, declared null and void; and any person or persons who shall hold, arrest, or return, or cause to be held, arrested, or returned, or in any manner aid in the arrest or return of any person or persons to a condition of peonage, shall, upon conviction, be punished by fine not less than one thousand nor more than five thousand dollars, or by imprisonment not less than one nor more than five years, or both, at the discretion of the court.

SEC. 2. *And be it further enacted,* That it shall be the duty of all persons in the military or civil service in the Territory of New Mexico to aid in the enforcement of the foregoing section of this act; and any person or persons who shall obstruct or attempt to obstruct, or in any way interfere with or prevent the enforcement of this act, shall be liable to the pains and penalties hereby provided; and any officer or other person in the military service of the United States who shall so offend, directly or indirectly, shall, on conviction before a court-martial, be dishonorably dismissed the service of the United States, and shall thereafter be ineligible to reappointment to any office of trust, honor, or profit under the Government.

APPROVED, March 2, 1867.

13

Treaty between the United States and the Navajos, Fort Sumner, 1868

In 1864, during a military campaign commanded by Christopher "Kit" Carson, the army marched the first large parties of what ultimately included more than 8,354 Navajos to Fort Sumner in the Pecos Valley. This Long Walk to the Bosque Redondo Reservation became a focal point in Navajo history. The Navajos eagerly signed the 1868 treaty permitting them to return to their beloved homeland, where they began the process of resettlement and of reconstruction of their shattered economy.

TREATY
between the
UNITED STATES OF AMERICA
and the
NAVAJO TRIBE OF INDIANS

1868 YĘĘDĄĄ'
NAABEEHO DINE'E BILAGAANA
YIŁ 'AHADA'DEEST'ANĘĘ

CONCLUDED JUNE 1, 1868.
RATIFICATION ADVISED JULY 25, 1868.
PROCLAIMED AUGUST 12, 1868.

ANDREW JOHNSON
PRESIDENT OF THE UNITED STATES
OF AMERICA

TO ALL AND SINGULAR TO WHOM THESE PRESENTS SHALL COME, GREETING:

Whereas a Treaty was made and concluded at Fort Sumner, in the Territory of New Mexico, on the first day of June, in the year of our Lord one thousand eight hundred and sixty-eight, by and between Lieutenant General W.T. Sherman and Samuel F. Tappan, Commissioners, on the part of the United States, and Barboncito, Armijo, and other Chiefs and Headmen of the Navajo tribe of Indians, on the part of said Indians, and duly authorized thereto by them, which Treaty is in the words and figures following, to wit:

Articles of a Treaty and Agreement made and entered into at Fort Sumner, New Mexico, on the first day of June, one thousand eight hundred and sixty-eight, by and between the United States, represented by its Commissioners, Lieutenant-General W.T. Sherman and Colonel Samuel F. Tappan, of the one part, and the Navajo Nation or tribe of Indians, represented by their chiefs and head-men, duly authorized and empowered to act for the whole people of said nation or tribe, (the names of said chiefs and head-men being hereto subscribed,) of the other part, witness:

Díí tsosts'idiin dóó ba'ąą táá' nááhaiidą́ą́' Ya'iishjááshchilí hayíítką́ bijí Hwéeldigi Naabeehó dóó Bilagáana yee 'ahada'-deest'ánę́ę 'át'é. Diné 'ahada'deest'áanii t'éiyá Wáashindoon yá ndaal'a'ígíí siláago binant'a'í W. T. Sherman dóó Samuel T. Tappan dóó 'índa Naabeehó 'alą́ąji' naazíinii lá.. Jó díí t'áá 'ałtso bidine'é yá 'ádáát'įįd.

ARTICLE I.
Łáa'ii góne'.

From this day forward all war between the parties to this agreement shall forever cease. The Government of the United States desires peace, and its honor is hereby pledged to keep it. The Indians desire peace, and they now pledge their honor to keep it.

Díísh jį́įdóó náás hodeeshzhiizhgóó diné 'anaa' dandzinę́ę yóó' 'adeididoo'ááł. Wáashindoon 'anaa' doo yinízin da, 'éí biniinaa yee 'ádee hadoodzíí'. Naabeehó 'anaa' doo yinízin da, 'éí biniinaa yee 'ádee hadoodzíí'.

If bad men among the whites, or among other people subject to the authority of the United States, shall commit any wrong upon the person or property of the Indians, the United States will, upon proof made to the agent and forwarded to the Commissioner of Indian Affairs at Washington City, proceed at once to cause the offender to be arrested and punished according to the laws of the United States, and also to reimburse the injured persons for the loss sustained.

Bilagáana bąąhági 'át'íinii dóó t'áá háiida Naabeehó ła' 'atíyiilaa dóó binichǫ́'í yits'ą́ą́ 'atíyiilaago dóó diné 'atíbi'diilyaaígíí Naabeehó binant'a'í Bilagáanaaígíí t'áá 'aaníí bee 'ábi'dool'įįdii yee yił hodoolnih, 'áádóó bi'doosdlą́ągdo Bilagáana Naabeehó binant'a'í nilínę́ę Wáashindoondi 'Indin binant'a'í yił nááhodoolnih. 'Áko 'índa 'Indin binant'a'í Naabeehó 'atíyiilaa yę́ę bił ninoohdeeł didooniił dóó bił n'deedéelgo Wáashindoondę́ę́' bee haz'áanii bik'ehgo tí'hwiizhdooni, dóó diné 'atíjiilaa yę́ę bich'į' nináazh'doodlééł.

If bad men among the Indians shall commit a wrong or depredation upon the person or property of any one, white, black, or Indian, subject to the authority of the United States and at peace therewith, the Navajo tribe agree that they will, on proof made to their agent, and on notice by him, deliver up the wrongdoer to the United States, to be tried and punished according to its laws; and in case they wilfully refuse so to do, the person injured shall be reimbursed for his loss from the annuities or other moneys due or to become due to them under this treaty, or any others that may be made with the United States. And the President may prescribe such rules and regulations for ascertaining damages under this article as in his judgment may be proper; but no such damage shall be adjusted and paid until examined and passed upon by the Commissioner of Indian Affairs, and no one sustaining loss whilst violating, or because of his violating, the provisions of this treaty or the laws of the United States shall be reimbursed therefor.

Naabeehó bąąhági 'át'íinii díí Naabeehó dóó Wáάshindoon yił 'ahada'deest'áné̜ę hoł 'ílíinii Bilagáana dóó Naakaii Łizhinii dóó 'Indin t'áá háiida 'atíjiilaago Bilagáana Naabeehó yinant'a'í nlíinii bee bił hodoonih, dóó Bilagáana Naabeehó yinant'a'í nlíinii Naabeehó t'áá yíl'áá ńt'ę̜ę' yee yi'doołnih dóó 'índa diné bąąhági 'ádzaa yę̜ę dah didoodlóós dóó Wáάshindoondę̜ę' beehaz'áanii bik'ehgo baa náhódóot'įįł, dóó t'áá 'éí bik'ehgo tí-hwiizhdooni. Naabeehó t'áá yíl'áá ńt'ę̜ę' bi'ílnii' dóó diné bąąhági 'ádzaa yę̜ę yaa danichį̜go Wáάshindoondę̜ę' Naabeehó béeso bá ch'íhinidéhę̜ę díí Bilagáana dóó t'áá háiida 'atíbi'diilyaa yę̜ę ła' bá ninádoolghééł. Díí 'ahadazh'deest'ánę̜ędą́ą́ béeso bee hada'-iisdzi'ę̜ę dóó náás hodeeshzhiizhgóó haa'ída diné 'ahanáάda'-deest'ą́ągo béeso bee hanáάda'iisdzi'ígíí díí diné 'atíyiilaa yę̜ę bich'į̜' ninádoolghééł. Wáάshindoondi sitíinii díí diné yee 'atída'a-hil'inígíí naalkaahgo bibeehaz'áanii 'íidoolííł, ndi t'áadoo le'é diné yee 'atída'ahiilyaaii 'Indin binant'a'í neiskáá' dóó yee lá 'asłį̜'-go 'índa bik'é niná'doolghééł. Diné ła' bąąhági 'ájít'įįgo t'áá biláahji' 'atízhdiilyaa dóó 'atího'diilyaago doo hach'į̜' niná'doolghééł da.

ARTICLE II.

Naaki góne'.

The United States agrees that the following district of country, to wit: bounded on the north by the 37th degree of north latitude, south by an east and west line passing through the site of old Fort Defiance, in Cañon Bonito, east by the parallel of longitude which, if prolonged south, would pass through old Fort Lyon, or the Ojo-de-oso, Bear Spring, and west by a parallel of longitude about 109° 30' west of Greenwich, provided it embraces the outlet of the Cañon-de-Chilly, which cañon is to be all included in this reservation, shall be, and the same is hereby, set apart for the use and occupation of the Navajo tribe of Indians, and for such other friendly tribes or individual Indians as from time to time they may be willing, with the consent of the United States, to admit among them; and the United States agrees that no persons except those herein so authorized to do, and except such officers, soldiers, agents, and employés of the government, or of the Indians, as may be authorized to enter upon Indian reservations in discharge of duties imposed by law, or the orders of the President, shall ever be permitted to pass over, settle upon, or reside in, the territory described in this article.

Wáάshindoondéé' Naabeehó bináhásdzooígíí bee nihoot'á: Tóghée'dóó hahoodzo náhookǫsjigo Toohji', 'áádóó 'e'e'aahjigo Tsé Bii' Njisgaiji', 'áádóó nát'ą́ą́' Tóghée'ji'. Tséghi' t'áá bii' hahodiil'áá n̄t'éé̜' Naabeehó bikéyah dooleeł, dóó choidayooł'įi dooleeł. Naabeehó díí kéyah bee nihoot'ánígíí bikáa'gi 'ał'ǫǫ 'ana'í ła' bił kéédahwiit'įi dooleeł daznízingo 'éí t'áá 'ákót'é, ndi 'átsé Wáάshindoon bee bi'doolnih. Díí kéyah náhásdzooígíí t'áá háiida 'ał'ǫǫ 'ana'í doo yikáá' ndoogáał da, t'áá hazhó'ó Wáάshindoon yá ndaal'a'ígíí dóó siláago t'éiyá yikáá' ndoogáał. Díí náhásdzooígíí 'ana'í t'áá háiida t'áadoo Wáάshindoon yee lá 'ałeehí doo bikáá' nizhdoogáał da.

ARTICLE III.

Táá' góne'·

The United States agrees to cause to be built, at some point within said reservation, where timber and water may be convenient, the following buildings: a warehouse, to cost not exceeding twenty-five hundred dollars; an agency building for the residence of the agent, not to cost exceeding three thousand dollars; a carpenter-shop and blacksmith-shop, not to cost exceeding one thousand dollars each; and a schoolhouse and chapel, so soon as a sufficient number of children can be induced to attend school, which shall not cost to exceed five thousand dollars.

Díí Naabeehó bináhásdzooígíí bikáa'gi tó dóó tsin dahólǫǫgi kin ła' 'ádadoolníił. Jó 'éí Wáάshindoon binaalghe'é báhooghan. Díí kinígíí naadiin 'ashdladi mííl béeso dóó nóghohji' doo bik'é 'ádoolníił da. 'Áádóó kin bighi'dóó nahat'áa dooleełii dóó t'áá 'éí Bilagáana Naabeehó binant'a'í nilíinii yii' bighan dooleeł, 'éí kinígíí táadi mííl béeso dóó nóghohji' doo bik'é 'ádoolníił da. 'Áádóó kin tsin neheshjíí' báhooghan dóó kin tsinaabąąs bighi' 'ándaal'ínígíí dóó bighi' 'atsid dooleełii 'ádadoolníił. Díí kinígíí t'áálá'í ní'ánigo t'áálahádi mííl béeso dóó nóghohji' doo bik'é 'ádoolníił da. 'Áádóó kin bighi' 'ólta' dooleełii dóó sodizin báhooghan dooleełii, ndi díí kinígíí 'áłchíní t'áá łá 'ólta'ji' ndahaas'nilgo t'éiyá 'ádoolníił. Díí kinígíí 'ashdladi mííl béeso dóó nóghohji' doo bik'é hadidooníił da.

ARTICLE IV.

Díí' góne'.

The United States agrees that the agent for the Navajos shall make his home at the agency building; that he shall reside among them, and shall keep an office open at all times for the purpose of prompt and diligent inquiry into such matters of complaint by or against the Indians as may be presented for investigation, as also for the faithful discharge of other duties enjoined by law. In all cases of depredation on person or property he shall cause the evidence to be taken in writing and forwarded, together with his finding, to the Commissioner of Indian Affairs, whose decision shall be binding on the parties to this treaty.

Wááshindoondǫ́ǫ́' Naabeehó binant'a'í nilíinii díí kin bighi'dóó nahat'á biniighé 'ályaa yę́ę́gi bighan dooleeł dóó Naabeehó yił kéédahat'į̇ dooleeł, dóó kin bighi' naaltsoos 'ájíł'ínígíí t'áá 'áłaji' 'qq deet'ą́ą́ dooleeł, 'áko Naabeehó t'áá tsį̇łgo choo'į̇ ndayiiłdeełigíí dóó t'áá tsį̇łgo hane' ndei'áhígíí bá baa ńjit'į̇ dooleeł. Díí Naabeehó binant'a'í jílíinii t'áá 'áłaji' haghangi jizdáa dooleeł 'áko Naabeehó 'atída'ahil'ínígíí dóó binichǫ́'í 'ałts'ą́ą́' 'atídeił'ínígíí bá njiłkaah dóó baa ńjit'į̇ dooleeł. T'áá 'ádǫǫh dahast'ą́ą́ shį̇ bá njiskáá' dóó naaltsoos bikáá' 'ázhdoolííł dóó 'Indin binant'a'í bich'į̇' 'azhdoo'ał. 'Indin binant'a'í t'áá 'ádíiniidgi bizh'doolííł, t'áá 'ałch'ishji díí diné 'ahada'deest'ánígíí·

ARTICLE V.

'Ashdla' góne'.

If any individual belonging to said tribe, or legally incorporated with it, being the head of a family, shall desire to commence farming, he shall have the privilege to select, in the presence and with the assistance of the agent then in charge, a tract of land within said reservation, not exceeding one hundred and sixty acres in extent, which tract, when so selected, certified, and recorded in the "land-book" as herein described, shall cease to be held in common, but the same may be occupied and held in the exclusive possession of the person selecting it, and of his family, so long as he or they may continue to cultivate it.

Naabeehó t'áá háiida dóó t'áá háiida beehaz'áanii bik'ehgo Naabeehó yitah níyáá shį̇ ba'áłchíní hólǫ́ǫgo dóó k'éé'díshdléeh dooleeł niizį̇'go kéyah ła' néididoo'áałgo bee hoo'a'. Kéyah łahgo náhozhdii'aahgo Naabeehó binant'a'í háká 'adoolghoł dóó binááł kéyah náhodizhdoo'ááł. Díí kéyahígíí náhásdzo hayázhí t'ááłáhádi neeznádiin dóó ba'qq hastą́diin náhásdzo doo biláahgo ńdizhdoo'ááł da. Kéyah nízhdii'ą́ą́ dóó yoołkááł bijį̇ góne' kéyah nízhdii'ánígíí dóó kéyah 'ákwii si'ánígíí dóó Naabeehó binant'a'í yee lá 'asłíi'go 'inda **Kéyah Binaaltsoos** há bikáá' 'ádoolnííł. Há 'ákóolyaa dóó díí kéyahígíí t'áá sáhí ha'áłchíní bił bee hóhólníih dooleeł t'áadoo k'éézhdoodlá bijíiji'. Bikáá' doo k'éézhdoodláa dago Naabeehó t'áá bíhólníhígíí kéyah yinízinii náánábíí' dooleeł.

Any person over eighteen years of age, not being the head of a family, may in like manner select, and cause to be certified to him or her for purposes of cultivation, a quantity of land, not exceeding eighty acres in extent, and thereupon be entitled to the excusive possession of the same as above directed.

Naabeehó tseebííts'áadah binááhaigo dóó ba'áłchíní 'ádin go kéyah ła' bikáá' k'éé'díshdléeh dooleeł niizíi'go díí diné ba'áłchíní dahólónígíí kéyah baa dahideest'ánígi 'át'éego kéyah haa hodidoot'ááł, ndi náhásdzo hayázhí tseebídiindi náhásdzogo haa didoot'ááł, dóó 'inda naaltsoos bikáa'go há hasht'e' nináádooltsos.

For each tract of land so selected a certificate containing a description thereof, and the name of the person selecting it, with a certificate endorsed thereon, that the same has been recorded, shall be delivered to the party entitled to it by the agent, after the same shall have been recorded by him in a book to be kept in his office, subject to inspection, which said book shall be known as the ''Navajo land-book.''

Naabeehó t'áá kéyah néidii'ą́ą́ shíi naaltsoos baa dooltsos. Díí naaltsoosígíí kéyah yaa halne'go dóó Naabeehó binant'a'í bízhi' bikáá', dóó kéyah baa deet'áanii bízhi' bikáa'go haa dooltsos, dóó náánáła' naaltsoos t'éiyá díí Naabeehó binant'a'í nilíinii bighandi t'áá 'ákót'éego kéyah yaa halne'go si'ą́ą́ dooleeł, 'áko t'áá naaltsoos dínéesh'íił nízin shíi yidínóoł'íiłgo bee hoo'a'. Díí naaltsoosígíí **Naabeehó Bikéyah Binaaltsoos** gholghéego yééji'.

The President may at any time order a survey of the reservation, and when so surveyed, Congress shall provide for protecting the rights of said settlers in their improvements, and may fix the character of the title held by each.

The United States may pass such laws on the subject of alienation and descent of property between the Indians and their descendants as may be thought proper.

Wááshindoondi sitíinii t'áá hoolzhishgi Naabeehó kéyah ńdayiizlá'ą́ą Wááshindoondę́ę́' kéyah yindaalnishígíí yich'i̜' yidooł'aał. Díí kéyah yindaalnishígíí kéyah náhaasdlá'ą́ą 'ałtso naaltsoos yikáá' ndeiznilgo, dóó Wááshindoondi dah ńdinibįįhígíí yee lá da'asłíi' dóó beehaz'áanii 'ádayiilaago kéyah náhaasdlá'ą́ą naaltsoos bá ch'ihidínóodah, 'áko 'inda náás hodeeshzhiizhgóó háadi da diné kéyah ńdayiizlá'ígíí náánáłahdę́ę́' diné doo biyaa

haidoo'áał da. Kólyaa dóó diné kéyah ńdajiizlá'ígíí hakéyah binaaltsoos t'áá ndajijaah dooleeł. Kéyah bąąh 'ádahasdįįdígíí dóó
kéyah 'ahaa ndajiilniihígíí biniighé Wáąshindoon t'áá bił yá'á-
t'ééh góne' yee beehaz'áanii 'íidoolíiłgo bá hoo'a'.

ARTICLE VI.
Hastání góne'.

In order to insure the civilization of the Indians entering into this treaty, the
necessity of education is admitted, especially of such of them as may be
settled on said agricultural parts of this reservation, and they therefore pledge
themselves to compel their children, male and female, between the ages of six
and sixteen years, to attend school; and it is hereby made the duty of the
agent for said Indians to see that this stipulation is strictly complied with; and
the United States agrees that, for every thirty children between said ages who
can be induced or compelled to attend school, a house shall be provided, and
a teacher competent to teach the elementary branches of an English education
shall be furnished, who will reside among said Indians, and faithfully
discharge his or her duties as a teacher.
The provisions of this article to continue for not less than ten years.

Nááś hodeeshzhiizhgóó Naabeehó 'íhoo'aahígíí bééhózingo yee, nááś didookah biniighé 'ólta' 'ádahoolyaa, dóó 'índa k'éé'-
dílghééh yee dahináa dooleełígíí t'áá 'íighisíí 'íhoo'aah bá yá'á-
t'ééh. 'Éí biniinaa kwe'é Naabeehó yee 'ádee hadadoodzíí'. Naabeehó ba'áłchíní 'at'ééké dóó 'ashiiké hastą́ą́ béédááhaaígíídóó
deigo hastą́'áadah béédááhaiji' t'áá 'ałtso 'ólta'ji' ndahidoo'nił.
Bilagáana Naabeehó binant'a'í nilínígíí díí 'áłchíní 'ólta'ji' nihe'-
níłígíí honaanish dooleeł, 'áko Naabeehó ba'áłchíní 'ólta' biniighé yee 'ádee hadahideesdzí'ę́ę yida'doolííł. 'Áłchíní tádiin yil-
t'éego 'ólta'ji' t'áá nihe'nííł bik'eh Bilagáana bá'ólta'í dóó kin bii'
'ólta' dooleełii nishóhoot'eeh dooleeł. Bá'ólta'í Bilagáanak'ehgo
t'áá 'íighisíí 'á 'ádaat'é ndahalinígíí t'éiyá bínazh'niłtin dooleeł.
Díí báda'ólta'ígíí Naabeehó yitahgi dabighan dooleeł, dóó honaanish danlíinii t'áá 'íighisíí bidazhdiilkaal dooleeł.

ARTICLE VII.
Tsosts'id góne'.

When the head of a family shall have selected lands and received his
certificate as above directed, and the agent shall be satisfied that he intends in
good faith to commence cultivating the soil for a living, he shall be entitled to
receive seeds and agricultural implements for the first year, not exceeding in
value one hundred dollars, and for each succeeding year he shall continue to
farm, for a period of two years, he shall be entitled to receive seeds and
implements to the value of twenty-five dollars.

Naabeehó ba'áłchíní hólóonii kéyah bikáá' k'éézh'dídlééh biniighé nízhdii'ą́ą́ dóó kéyah binaaltsoos shíjoost'e'go díí kéyah- ígíí bina'anish bizhdiilkaal dóó t'ááłáhádi názh'neest'ą́ągo k'eel- ghéí dóó bee na'anishí Wááshindoon t'áá 'ájíík'eh. haa yidoonił. Díí bee na'anishí yígíí neeznádiin béeso dóó nóghohji' doo bą́ą́h 'adooleeł da. K'eelghéí dóó bee na'anishí haa yí'nil dóó bik'iji' nizhónígo kéyah bikáá' k'éézh'dídléehgo naaki nááhaigo bee na'- anishí dóó k'eelghéí naadį́į́ 'ashdla' béeso bíighahgo t'áá 'ájíík'eh haa náádoo'nił.

ARTICLE VIII.
Tseebíí góne'.

In lieu of all sums of money or other annuities provided to be paid to the Indians herein named under any treaty or treaties heretofore made, the United States agrees to deliver at the agency-house on the reservation herein named, on the first day of September of each year for ten years, the following articles, to wit:

Díí k'ad 'ahadazh'deest'ánígíí t'ah bítséedi 'ahadazh'dees- t'ą́ągo Wááshindoondéé' béeso Naabeehó bá ch'íhinidéeh dooleeł ho'doo'niidę́ę k'ad 'éí béesoígíí bikék'ehji' t'áadoo le'é Wááshin- doondéé' t'áá nináháháán bik'eh Bini'ant'ą́ą́tsoh ńdízídígíí ha- néílkááh góne' Naabeehó bá nehegeehgo neeznáá ńdoohah·

Such articles of clothing, goods, or raw materials in lieu thereof, as the agent may make his estimate for, not exceeding in value five dollars per Indian—each Indian being encouraged to manufacture their own clothing, blankets, etc.; to be furnished with no article which they can manufacture themselves. And, in order that the Commissioner of Indian Affairs may be able to estimate properly for the articles herein named, it shall be the duty of the agent each year to forward to him a full and exact census of the Indians, on which the estimate from year to year can be based.

Bilagáana Naabeehó yinant'a'í nilíinii díí t'áadoo le'é ne- hegeeh dooleełígíí Wááshindoon yínáyóki' dooleeł. Jó 'éí 'éé' dóó t'áadoo le'é 'éé' dóó beeldléí bee 'ádaal'ínígíí lá. Naabeehó bi- nant'a'í Wááshindoongóó t'áadoo le'é ńjóki'go Naabeehó t'ááłá'í sizínígíí 'ashdla' béeso bíighahgo t'áadoo le'é bá ńjóki' dooleeł. Wááshindoondéé' 'ádaaníigo bíni' Naabeehó t'áá bí bi'éé' 'ádeił'į. T'áadoo le'é Naabeehó t'áá bí 'ádeił'íinii t'éiyá doo nehegeeh da dooleeł. Naabeehó binant'a'í t'áá nináháháán bik'eh Naabeehó 'ánéelt'e'gi Wááshindoonji' baa náhojilnih dooleeł, dóó t'áá 'éí binahji' t'áadoo le'é Naabeehó t'áá bee néelt'e'go nehegeeh doo-leeł.

And in addition to the articles herein named, the sum of ten dollars for each person entitled to the beneficial effects of this treaty shall be annually appropriated for a period of ten years, for each person who engages in farming or mechanical pursuits, to be used by the Commissioner of Indian Affairs in the purchase of such articles as from time to time the condition and necessities of the Indians may indicate to be proper; and if within the ten years at any time it shall appear that the amount of money needed for clothing, under the article, can be appropriated to better uses for the Indians named herein, the Commissioner of Indian Affairs may change the appropriation to other purposes, but in no event shall the amount of this appropriation be withdrawn or discontinued for the period named, provided they remain at peace. And the President shall annually detail an officer of the Army to be present and attest the delivery of all the goods herein named to the Indians, and he shall inspect and report on the quantity and quality of the goods and the manner of their delivery.

Díí t'áadoo le'é nehegeehígíí bił Naabeehó dá'ák'ehgi na'-anish t'áá 'íighisíí yidadiilkaalii t'áá nináháháah bik'eh t'áadoo le'é neeznáá béeso bíighahgo baa ha'nííł dooleeł. T'áá nináhá-háah bik'eh díí neeznáá béesoígíí 'Indin binant'a'í t'áadoo le'é Naabeehó yinízinii yee yá nayiiłniih dooleeł. T'áadoo neeznáá náháhí Naabeehó bi'éé' t'áá bí 'ádeił'į daazlį́į' dóó bik'iji' díí bée-so yę́ę t'áadoo le'é t'áá 'íighisíí yídin danlíinii bá nahidoonih. Díí béesoígíí t'áadoo neeznáá náháhí t'áadoo biniinaanígóó doo 'áá-doolzįįł da, t'áá hazhó'ó Naabeehó 'anaa' náádaniidzį́į'go t'éiyá 'áádoolzįįł. T'áá nináháháah bik'eh t'áadoo le'é Naabeehó bá ni-nágéehgo Wááshindoondę́ę' siláago binant'a'í ła' yiniighé nádáah dooleeł. Díí siláago binant'a'í yígíí t'áadoo le'é ninágéhígíí hanéí-si' dooleeł dóó Naabeehó bitaaná'nihgóó hanéisi' dooleeł, 'áko Wááshindoondi díí t'áadoo le'é niná'nihígíí 'áneelt'e' dóó bą́ą́h 'azlį́į'gi bił bééhózingo nináhádáah dooleeł.

ARTICLE IX.
Náhást'éí góne'.

In consideration of the advantages and benefits conferred by this treaty, and the many pledges of friendship by the United States, the tribes who are parties to this agreement hereby stipulate that they will relinquish all right to occupy any territory outside their reservation, as herein defined, but retain the right to hunt on any unoccupied lands contiguous to their reservation, so long as the large game may range thereon in such numbers as to justify the chase; and they, the said Indians, further expressly agree:

Wááshindoon t'áadoo le'é Naabeehó bá yá'át'éehii yaa yi-diní'ánígíí binahji' díí Naabeehó bá náhásdzooígíí binaagóó ké-yahígíí doo baa dajíchį' da dooleeł. Ndi díí náhásdzooígíí tł'óó'-góó kéyah t'áá bíni' naaznilígíí bikáá'góó ndaalzheeh dooleeł. Jó 'éí t'áadoo le'é hada'azheehígíí bikáá' hólǫ́ǫgo t'éiyá 'ákót'ée doo-leeł. 'Áádóó náánáłahgóó t'áadoo le'é bee 'ádee hadahizhdees-dzíí'. Jó 'éí:

1st. That they will make no opposition to the construction of railroads now being built or hereafter to be built across the continent.

1. Béésh ńt'i' kéyah t'áá dah si'ą́ą́ ńt'ę́ę́' ha'naa dilt'éehgo dóó náás hodeeshzhiizhgóó ha'át'éegi da ła' náádílt'éehgo doo bi-ch'ą́ą́h nizhdookah da.

2d. That they will not interfere with the peaceful construction of any railroad not passing over their reservation as herein defined.

2. Ha'át'éegi da Naabeehó bá náhásdzooígíí bits'ą́ądi béésh dilt'éehgo doo bich'ą́ą́h nizhdookah da.

3d. That they will not attack any persons at home or travelling, nor molest or disturb any wagon-trains, coaches, mules or cattle belonging to the people of the United States, or to persons friendly therewith.

3. Ha'át'éegi da diné nizhónígo bighangi sidáago dóó yigáał go da, dóó tsinaabąąs naalghéhé ła' dóó diné ła' yooghéełgo doo 'atízhdoolííł da. Diné Wááshindoondę́ę́' hoot'áałii bił 'ííiinii bini-chǫ́'í dóó bibéégashii dóó bidzaanééz doo 'atízhdoolííł da.

4th. That they will never capture or carry off from the settlements women or children.

4. Kin dah naazhjaa'dóó 'áłchíní dóó sáanii doo yóó' 'ada-hizhdoojih da.

5th. They will never kill or scalp white men, nor attempt to do them harm.

5. Ha'át'éegi da Bilagáana doo jidiyoołhéeł da, dóó bitsiiziz doo 'ázhdoolííł da, dóó 'atídoolnííł doo bee bąąh tsízdookos da.

6th. They will not in future oppose the construction of railroads, wagon-roads, mail stations, or other works of utility or necessity which may be ordered or permitted by the laws of the United States; but should such roads or other works be constructed on the lands of their reservation, the Government will pay the tribe whatever amount of damage may be assessed by three disinterested commissioners to be appointed by the President for that purpose, one of said commissioners to be a chief or head-man of the tribe.

6. Náás hodeeshzhiizhgóó ha'át'éegi da béésh ńt'i' 'álnéehgo dóó 'atiin 'áhálnééh dóó naaltsoos ndaagéhígíí báhooghan 'álnéehgo dóó t'áadoo le'é t'áá 'íighisíí choo'íinii 'álnéehgo Wááshindoondéé' beehaz'áanii bik'ehgo doo bich'ą́ą́h nizhdookah da. Díí kódaat'éhígíí Naabeehó bináhásdzo bikáa'gi 'álnéehgo Naabeehó bik'é bich'į' ń'doolghééł. Naabeehó bináhásdzooígíí bikáá' t'áadoo le'é 'álnéehgo Wááshindoondi sitíinii diné t'áá háiida yich'į' yidooł'aał dóó neidoołkah dóó 'índa kéyah bikáá' t'áadoo le'é 'álnéhígíí bą́ą́h 'ílį́į́ góne' yee hadoodzih. J'ó díí Wááshindoondi sitíinii yá naal'a'ígíí Naabeehó 'alą́ą́ji' sizíinii ła' dooleeł.

7th. They will make no opposition to the military posts or roads now established, or that may be established, not in violation of treaties heretofore made or hereafter to be made with any of the Indian tribes.

7. Hool'áágóó ha'át'éegi da siláago nínínáago dóó k'ad 'atiin 'ádahoolyaaígíí dóó ła' 'ánáádabi'niilyaago doo bich'ą́ą́h nizhdookah da, dóó 'índa díí k'ad 'ahadazh'deest'ánígíí dóó hool'áágóó haa'í da náánáła' 'ał'ąą 'ana'í bił 'ahanáádazh'deest'ą́ągo doo k'ídazhdoonish da.

ARTICLE X.
Neeznání góne'.

No future treaty for the cession of any portion or part of the reservation herein described, which may be held in common, shall be of any validity or force against said Indians unless agreed to and executed by at least three-fourths of all the adult male Indians occupying or interested in the same; and no cession by the tribe shall be understood or construed in such manner as to deprive, without his consent, any individual member of the tribe of his rights to any tract of land selected by him as provided in article 5 of this treaty.

Kodóó náás hodeeshzhiizhgóó háadida doo díí 'ahada'deest'ánígi 'át'éego ła' bee 'ahanááda'didiit'áał da, dóó 'índa hool'áágóó doo háadida Naabeehó náánáła' 'ana'í doo kéyah yaa yididoo'áał da, t'áá hazhó'ó Naabeehó bináhásdzooígíí bighi' diné kéédahat'ínígíí 'ałníí' biláahgo yee lá da'asłį́į'go t'éiyá· Kéyahígíí t'áá háiida 'ana'í ła' baa deet'ą́ą ndi díí kéyahígíí bikáa'gi diné kéyah ndayiizláá' dóó kéyah binaaltsoos bee dahólǫ́ǫgo bikéyahígíí doo bits'ádoolts'ił da, 'azhą́ Naabeehó t'áá yíl'áá ńt'ę́ę́' 'ałníí' biláahgo yee lá da'asłį́į' ndi.

ARTICLE XI.
Ła'ts'áadah góne'.

The Navajos also hereby agree that at any time after the signing of these presents they will proceed in such manner as may be required of them by the agent, or by the officer charged with their removal, to the reservation herein provided for, the United States paying for their subsistence en route, and providing a reasonable amount of transportation for the sick and feeble.

Díí k'ad bee 'ahadazh'deest'ánígíí t'áá 'ałtso ła' yidzaaí t'áá 'áko Naabeehó bikéyahgóó Bilagáana Naabeehó yinant'a'í nilíinii bik'ehgo nikéédahizhdoo'nééł, dóó ch'iyáán bikiin nikéédahizhdoo'néłígíí dóó tsinaabąqs Naabeehó bąqh dah ndahaz'ánígíí dóó t'áadoo le'é doo yídaniłdzilígíí yee Wááshindoon yíká 'adoolghoł.

ARTICLE XII.
Naakits'áadah góne'.

It is further agreed by and between the parties to this agreement that the sum of one hundred and fifty thousand dollars appropriated or to be appropriated shall be disbursed as follows, subject to any conditions provided in the law, to wit:

Díí k'ad diné 'ahada'deest'ánígíí t'áá náánáłáhágo haz'ą bee 'ahanáádazh'deest'ą; jó 'éí Wááshindoondę́ę' béeso t'ááłáhádi neeznádiin dóó ba'ąą 'ashdladiindi mííl Naabeehó bá ch'ídínóodah dóó 'éí kót'éego choidoo'įįł:

1st. The actual cost of the removal of this tribe from the Bosque Redondo reservation to the reservation, say fifty thousand dollars.

1. Hwéeldidę́ę' nikééda'iiznáádóó nináda'iis'náaji' díí béeso yę́ę 'ashdladiindi mííl biighahgo bik'e ń'doo'nééł.

2d. The purchase of fifteen thousand sheep and goats, at a cost not to exceed thirty thousand dollars.

2. Dibé dóó tł'ízí 'ashdla'áadahdi mííl béeso biighahgo bee Naabeehó bá nahidoonih. Díí dibé dóó tł'ízí nahidoonihígíí tádiindi mííl béeso dóó nóghohji' doo bik'é ndoolghéeł da·

3d. The purchase of five hundred beef cattle and a million pounds of corn, to be collected and held at the military post nearest the reservation, subject to the orders of the agent, for the relief of the needy during the coming winter.

3. Naabeehó béégashii 'ashdladi neeznádiingo bá nahidoonih, dóó naadą́ą́' t'áálą́hádi mííl ntsaaígíí bíighahgo dahidédlo'go bá nahidoonih. Díí ndahaaznii' dóó Naabeehó bikéyah bikáa'gi siláago dabighangi Naabeehó haigo choidayooł'į́į dooleeł biniighé bá sinil dooleeł.

4th. The balance, if any, of the appropriation to be invested for the maintenance of the Indians pending their removal, in such manner as the agent who is with them may determine.

4. Bilagáana Naabeehó binant'a'í nilíinii díí béeso yę́ę ła' ch'íníídee' ládą́ą́' t'áá bí yaa ntsékeesgo t'áadoo le'é Naabeehó bá yá'át'éehii yá neidiyoołnih, nikééda'iis'náa bijį́įji'.

5th. The removal of this tribe to be made under the supreme control and direction of the military commander of the Territory of New Mexico, and when completed, the management of the tribe to revert to the proper agent.

5. Hwéeldidóó dah ń'dii'náá dóó Naabeehó bikéyah bikáá' niná'iis'náaji' Yootó bináhásdzooígíí bighi'dóó siláago binant'a'í bik'ehgo nikéé'doo'nééł. Naabeehó bináhásdzo bii' ná'oo'náá dóó 'índa Bilagáana Naabeehó binant'a'í nilíinii bik'ehgo ch'í'dooldah

ARTICLE XIII.
Tááts'áadah góne'.

The tribe herein named, by their representatives, parties to this treaty, agree to make the reservation herein described their permanent home, and they will not as a tribe make any permanent settlement elsewhere, reserving the right to hunt on the lands adjoining the said reservation formerly called theirs, subject to the modifications named in this treaty and the orders of the commander of the department in which said reservation may be for the time being; and it is further agreed and understood by the parties to this treaty, that if any Navajo Indian or Indians shall leave the reservation herein described to settle elsewhere, he or they shall forfeit all the rights, privileges, and annuities conferred by the terms of this treaty; and it is further agreed by the parties to this treaty, that they will do all they can to induce Indians now away from reservations set apart for the exclusive use and occupation of the Indians, leading a nomadic life, or engaged in war against the people of the United States, to abandon such a life and settle permanently in one of the territorial reservations set apart for the exclusive use and occupation of the Indians.

Naabeehó dine'é gholghéii 'aláąji' naazínígíí k'ad kodóó hool'áágóó Naabeehó bá náhásdzooígíí t'éiyá bighi' kéédahat'įį dooleeł dóó háadi da doo tł'óó'góó ła' kódooníił da daaníigo yee 'ádee hadadeesdzíí'. Kéyah díí 'ahadazh'deest'ánígíí t'ah bítséedi Naabeehó daabíhę́ę bikáá' na'azheeh doo bee ha'oodzíí' da. Díí kéyahígíí bikáá' na'azheeh t'áá bee bá haz'ą́ą ndi beehaz'áanii bik'ehgo na'azheehgo bee hoo'a'.

Díí Naabeehó bá náhásdzooígíí tł'óó'góó Naabeehó haghan 'ádahojiilaaígíí t'áadoo le'é Naabeehó náhásdzo bighi'gi yee ńda'aldįįhígíí doo bee ńdazh'dooldįįł da. Díí diné 'ahada'deest'ánígíí hool'áágóó háadida náánáła' 'ana'í t'áá 'áłaji' tádadinééh dóó ndaabaahgo hazhó'ó nihináhásdzo díí nihí kééhwiit'ínígi 'át'éego kéédahooht'įį dooleeł dabizhdooniił.

In testimony of all which the said parties have hereunto, on this the first day of June, one thousand eight hundred and sixty-eight, at Fort Sumner, in the Territory of New Mexico, set their hands and seals.

Doodaatsaahii bi'dizhchį́įdóó t'ááłáhádi mííl dóó ba'ąą tseebíidi neeznádiin dóó ba'ąą hastą́diin dóó ba'ąą tseebíí náhááh góne' Ya'iishjááshchilí hayííłką́ bijį́į góne' Hwéeldidi bee 'ahadazh'deest'ánígíí nihízhi' bikáá' 'ádeiilyaa dóó bik'i ndadiniilnii'.

W.T. SHERMAN
Lieutenant-General, Indian Peace Commissioner.
S.F. TAPPAN,
Indian Peace Commissioner.
BARBONCITO, chief, his x mark.
ARMIJO, his x mark.
DELGADO.
MANUELITO, his x mark.
LARGO, his x mark.
HERRERO, his x mark.
CHIQUETO, his x mark.
MUERTO DE HOMBRE, his x mark.
HOMBRO, his x mark.
NARBONO, his x mark.
NARBONO SEGUNDO, his x mark.
GAÑADO MUCHO, his x mark.

Council:
RIQUO, his x mark.
JUAN MARTIN, his x mark.
SERGINTO, his x mark.
GRANDE, his x mark.
INOETENITO, his x mark.
MUCHACHOS MUCHO, his x mark.
CHIQUETO SEGUNDO, his x mark.

CABELLO AMARILLO, his x mark.
FRANCISCO, his x mark.
TORIVIO, his x mark.
DESDENDADO, his x mark.
JUAN, his x mark.
GUERO, his x mark.
GUGADORE, his x mark.
CABASON, his x mark.
BARBON SEGUNDO, his x mark.
CABARES COLORADOS, his x mark.

Attest:
Geo. W.G. Getty,
Colonel Thirty-seventh Infantry, Brevet Major-General U.S. Army.
B.S. Roberts,
Brevet Brigadier-General U.S. Army, Lieutenant-Colonel Third Cavalry.
J. Cooper Mckee,
Brevet Lieutenant-Colonel, Surgeon U.S. Army.
Theo. H. Dodd,
United States Indian Agent for Navajos.
Chas. McClure,
Brevet Major and Commissary of Subsistence, U.S. Army.
James F. Weeds,
Brevet Major and Assistant Surgeon, U.S. Army.
J.C. Sutherland,
Interpreter.
William Vaux,
Chaplain U.S. Army.

And whereas, the said treaty having been submitted to the Senate of the United States for its constitutional action thereon, the Senate did, on the twenty-fifth day of July, one thousand eight hundred and sixty-eight, advise and consent to the ratification of the same, by a resolution in the words and figures following, to wit:

In Executive Session, Senate of the United States,
July 25, 1868.

Resolved, (two-thirds of the senators present concurring,) That the Senate advise and consent to the ratification of the treaty between the United States and the Navajo Indians, concluded at Fort Sumner, New Mexico, on the first day of June, 1868.

Attest:

GEO. C. GORHAM,
Secretary,
By W.J. McDONALD,
Chief Clerk.

Now, therefore, be it known that I, Andrew Johnson, President of the United States of America, do, in pursuance of the advice and consent of the Senate, as expressed in its resolution of the twenty-fifth of July, one thousand eight hundred and sixty-eight, accept, ratify, and confirm the said treaty.

In testimony whereof, I have hereto signed my name, and caused the seal of the United States to be affixed.

Done at the City of Washington, this twelfth day of August, in the year of our Lord one thousand eight hundred and sixty-eight, and of the Independence of the United States of America the ninety-third.

ANDREW JOHNSON

By the President:
W. HUNTER,
Acting Secretary of State.

14

Governor Wallace's Proclamation of Amnesty in the Lincoln County War, 1878

The Lincoln County War, a rivalry between two economic groups, erupted into violence with the killing of John H. Tunstall in 1878. In retaliation Billy the Kid and others killed Sheriff William Brady, and ultimately an attack was launched against members of one faction who were barricaded in Alexander McSween's store. A United States government special investigator's report led to a presidential proclamation that Lincoln County was in a state of insurrection and to the removal of Governor William Axtell. The new governor, Lew Wallace, who became famous as the author of *Ben Hur,* issued this amnesty proclamation in an effort to end the bloodshed.

PROCLAMATION BY THE GOVERNOR
November 13, 1878

FOR the information of the people of the United States, and of the citizens of the Territory of New Mexico in especial, the undersigned announces that the disorders lately prevalent in Lincoln County in said Territory have been happily brought to an end. Persons having business and property interests therein, and who are themselves peaceably disposed, may go to and from that County without hindrance or molestation. Individuals resident there, but who have been driven away, or who from choice sought safety elsewhere, are invited to return, under assurance that ample measure have been taken, and are now and will be continued in force, to make them secure in person and property.

And that the people of Lincoln County may be helped more speedily to the management of their civil affairs, as contemplated by law, and to induce them to lay aside forever the divisions and feuds which, by national notoriety, have been so prejudicial to their locality and the whole Territory, the undersigned, by virtue of authority in him vested, further proclaims a general pardon for misdemeanors and offenses committed in said County of Lincoln against the laws of the said Territory, in connection with the aforesaid disorders, between the first day of February, eighteen hundred and seventy eight and the date of this proclamation.

And it is expressly understood that the foregoing pardon is upon the conditions and limitations following: It shall not apply except to officers of the United States army stationed in the said County during the said disorders, and to persons who, at the time of the commission of the offense or misdemeanor of which they may be accused, were, with good intent, resident

72

citizens of the said Territory, and who shall have hereafter kept the peace, and conducted themselves in all respects as becomes good citizens. Neither shall it be pleaded by any person in bar of conviction under indictment now found and returned for any such crimes or misdemeanors, nor operate the release of any party undergoing pains and penalties consequent upon sentence heretofore had for any crime or misdemeanor.

In witness whereof I have hereunto set my hand and caused the seal of the Territory of New Mexico to be affixed.

> Done at the City of Santa Fe,
> this thirteenth day of November,
> A.D. Eighteen hundred and
> seventy eight.
> LEWIS WALLACE
> Governor of New Mexico

By the Governor:
W.G. RITCH
Secretary

15

Enabling Act by Congress, 1910

In 1910 New Mexico had been a territory for sixty years, longer than any other area in the continental United States, and New Mexicans had sought statehood for a longer period. Repeated movements for statehood in the nineteenth century were defeated in the Congress as the issue of New Mexico statehood became enmeshed in national political issues, but the quest for statehood continued in the twentieth century with Bernard "Statehood" Rodey providing leadership. The Enabling Act of 1910 finally authorized New Mexicans to select a constitutional convention to prepare for an entry as an equal partner in the United States.

ENABLING ACT
for
NEW MEXICO

(June 20, 1910)

Section 1. The qualified electors of the Territory of New Mexico are hereby authorized to vote for and choose delegates to form a constitutional convention for said territory for the purpose of framing a constitution for the proposed State of New Mexico. Said convention shall consist of one hundred delegates; and the governor, chief justice, and secretary of said territory shall apportion the delegates to be thus selected, as nearly as may be, equitably among the several counties thereof in accordance with the voting population, as shown by the vote cast at the election for delegate in congress in said territory in nineteen hundred and eight: Provided, That in the event that any new counties shall have been added after said election, the apportionment for delegates shall be made proportionate to the vote cast within the various precincts contained in the area of such new counties so created, and the proportionate number of delegates so apportioned shall be deducted from the original counties out of which such counties shall have been created.

The governor of said territory shall, within thirty days after the approval of this act, by proclamation, in which the aforesaid apportionment of delegates to the convention shall be fully specified and announced, order an election of the delegates aforesaid on a day designated by him in said proclamation, not earlier than sixty nor later than ninety days after the approval of this act. Such election for delegates shall be held and conducted, the returns made, and the certificates of persons elected to such convention issued, as nearly as may be, in the same manner as is prescribed by the laws of said territory regulating elections therein of members of the legislature existing at the time of the last election of said members of the legislature; and the provisions of said laws in all respects, including the qualifications of electors and registration, are hereby made applicable to the election herein provided for; and said convention, when so called to order and organized, shall be the sole judge of the election and qualifications of its own members. Qualifications to entitle persons to vote on the ratification or rejection of the constitution formed by said convention when said constitution shall be submitted to the people of said territory hereunder shall be the same as the qualifications to entitle persons to vote for delegates to said convention.

Sec. 2. The delegates to the convention thus elected shall meet in the hall of the house of representatives in the capital of the Territory of New Mexico at twelve o'clock noon on the fourth Monday after their election, and they shall receive compensation for the period they actually are in session, but not for more than sixty days in all. After organization they shall declare on behalf of the people of said proposed state that they adopt the Constitution of the United States, whereupon the said convention shall be, and is hereby, authorized to form a constitution and provide for a state government for said proposed state, all in the manner and under the conditions contained in this act. The constitution shall be republican in form and make no distinction in civil or political rights on account of race or color, and shall not be repugnant to the Constitution of the United States and the principles of the Declaration of Independence.

And said convention shall provide, by an ordinance irrevocable without the consent of the United States and the people of said state—

First. That perfect toleration of religious sentiment shall be secured, and that no inhabitant of said state shall ever be molested in person or property on account of his or her mode of religious worship; and that polygamous or plural marriages, or polygamous cohabitation, and the sale, barter, or giving of intoxicating liquors to Indians and the introduction of liquors into Indian country, which term shall also include all lands now owned or occupied by the Pueblo Indians of New Mexico, are forever prohibited.

Second. That the people inhabiting said proposed state do agree and declare that they forever disclaim all right and title to the unappropriated and ungranted public lands lying within the boundaries thereof and to all lands lying within said boundaries owned or held by any Indian or Indian tribes the right or title to which shall have been acquired through or from the United States or any prior sovereignty, and that until the title of such Indian or Indian tribes shall have been extinguished the same shall be and remain subject to the disposition and under the absolute jurisdiction and control of the congress of the United States; that the lands and other property belonging to citizens of the United States residing without the said state shall never be taxed at a higher rate than the lands and other property belonging to residents thereof; that no taxes shall be imposed by the state upon lands or property therein belonging to or which may hereafter be acquired by the United States or reserved for its use; but nothing herein, or in the ordinance herein provided for, shall preclude the said state from taxing, as other lands and other property are taxed, any lands and other property outside of an Indian reservation owned or held by any Indian, save and except such lands as have been granted or acquired as aforesaid or as may be granted or confirmed to any Indian or Indians under any act of congress, but said ordinance shall provide that all such lands shall be exempt from taxation by said state so long and to such extent as congress has prescribed or may hereafter prescribe.

Third. That the debts and liabilities of said Territory of New Mexico and the debts of the counties thereof which shall be valid and subsisting at the time of the passage of this act shall be assumed and paid by said proposed state, and that said state shall, as to all such debts and liabilities, be subrogated to all the rights, including rights of indemnity and reimbursement, existing in favor of said territory or of any of the several counties thereof at the time of the passage of this act: Provided, That nothing in this act shall be construed as validating or in any manner legalizing any territorial, county, municipal, or other bonds, obligations, or evidences of indebtedness of said territory or the counties or municipalities thereof which now are or may be invalid or illegal at the time said proposed state is admitted, nor shall the legislature of said proposed state pass any law in any manner validating or legalizing the same.

Fourth. That provision shall be made for the establishment and maintenance of a system of public schools, which shall be open to all the children of said state and free from sectarian control, and that said schools shall always be conducted in English.

Fifth. That said state shall never enact any law restricting or abridging the right of suffrage on account of race, color, or previous condition of servitude.

Sixth. That the capital of said state shall, until changed by the electors voting at an election provided for by the legislature of said state for that purpose, be at the city of Santa Fe, but no election shall be called or provided for prior to the thirty-first day of December, nineteen hundred and twenty-five.

Seventh. That there be and are reserved to the United States, with full acquiescense of the state, all rights and powers for the carrying out of the provisions by the United States of the act of congress entitled "An act appropriating the receipts from the sale and disposal of public lands in certain states and territories to the construction of irrigation works for the reclamation of arid lands," approved June seventeenth, nineteen hundred and two, and acts amendatory thereof or supplementary thereto, to the same extent as if said state had remained a territory.

Eighth. That whenever hereafter any of the lands contained within Indian reservations or allotments in said proposed state shall be allotted, sold, reserved, or otherwise disposed of, they shall be subject for a period of twenty-five years after such allotment, sale, reservation, or other disposal to all the laws of the United States prohibiting the introduction of liquor into the Indian country; and the terms "Indian" and "Indian country" shall include the Pueblo Indians of New Mexico and the lands now owned or occupied by them.

Ninth. That the state and its people consent to all and singular the provisions of this act concerning the lands hereby granted or confirmed to the state, the terms and conditions upon which said grants and confirmations are made, and the means and manner of enforcing such terms and conditions, all in every respect and particular as in this act provided.

All of which ordinance described in this section shall, by proper reference, be made a part of any constitution that shall be formed hereunder, in such terms as shall positively preclude the making by any future constitutional amendment of any change or abrogation of the said ordinance in whole or in part without the consent of congress. (As amended Aug. 21, 1911, 37 Stat. 42, J.R. No. 8.)

Sec. 3. When said constitution shall be formed as aforesaid the convention forming the same shall provide for the submission of said constitution to the people of New Mexico for ratification at an election which shall be held on a day named by said convention not earlier than sixty nor later than ninety days after said convention adjourns, at which election the qualified voters of New

Mexico shall vote directly for or against said constitution and for or against any provisions thereof separately submitted. The returns of said election shall be made by the election officers direct to the secretary of the Territory of New Mexico at Santa Fe, who, with the governor and the chief justice of said territory, shall constitute a canvassing board, and they, or any two of them, shall meet at said City of Santa Fe on the third Monday after said election and shall canvass the same. If a majority of the legal votes cast at said election shall reject the constitution, the said canvassing board shall forthwith certify said result to the governor of said territory, together with the statement of votes cast upon the question of the ratification or rejection of said constitution and also a statement of the votes cast for or against such provisions thereof as were separately submitted to the voters at said election; whereupon the governor of said territory shall, by proclamation, order the constitutional convention to reassemble at a date not later than twenty days after the receipt by said governor of the documents showing the rejection of the constitution by the people, and thereafter a new constitution shall be framed and the same proceedings shall be taken in regard thereto in like manner as if said constitution were being originally prepared for submission and submitted to the people.

Sec. 4. When said constitution and such provisions thereof as have been separately submitted shall have been duly ratified by the people of New Mexico as aforesaid a certified copy of the same shall be submitted to the president of the United States and to congress for approval, together with the statement of the votes cast thereon and upon any provisions thereof which were separately submitted to and voted upon by the people. And if congress and the president approves said constitution and the said separate provisions thereof, or, if the president approves the same and congress fails to disapprove the same during the next regular session thereof, then and in that event the president shall certify said facts to the governor of New Mexico, who shall, within thirty days after the receipt of said notification from the president of the United States, issue his proclamation for the election of the state and county officers, the members of the state legislature and representatives in congress, and all other officers provided for in said constitution, all as hereinafter provided; said election to take place not earlier than sixty days nor later than ninety days after said proclamation by the governor of New Mexico ordering the same.

Sec. 5. Said constitutional convention shall, by ordinance, provide that in case of the ratification of said constitution by the people, and in case the president of the United States and congress approve the same, or in case the president approves the same and congress fails to act in its next regular session, all as hereinbefore provided, an election shall be held at the time named in the proclamation of the governor of New Mexico, provided for in the preceding section, at which election officers for a full state government, including a governor, members of the legislature, two representatives in congress, to be elected at large from said state, and such other officers as such constitutional convention shall prescribe, shall be chosen by the people. Such election shall be held, the returns thereof made, canvassed, and certified to by the secretary of said territory in the same manner as in this act prescribed for the making of the returns, the canvassing and certification of the same of the election for the ratification or rejection of said constitution, as hereinbefore provided, and the qualifications of voters at said election for all state officers, members of the legislature, county officers, and representatives in congress, and other officers prescribed by said constitution shall be made the same as the qualifications of voters at the election for the ratification or rejection of said constitution as hereinbefore provided. When said election of said state and county officers, members of the legislature, and representatives in congress, and other officers above provided for shall be held and the returns thereof made, canvassed, and certified as hereinbefore provided, the governor of the territory of New Mexico shall certify the result of said election, as canvassed and certified as herein provided, to the president of the United States, who thereupon shall immediately issue his proclamation announcing the result of said election so ascertained, and upon the issuance of said proclamation by the president of the United States the proposed state of New Mexico shall be deemed admitted by congress into the union, by virtue of this act, on an equal footing with the other states. Until the issuance of said proclamation by the president of the United States, and until the said state is so admitted into the union and said officers are elected and qualified under the provisions of the constitution, the county and territorial officers of said territory, including the delegate in congress thereof elected at the general election in nineteen hundred and eight, shall continue to discharge the duties of their respective offices in and for said territory: Provided, That no session of the territorial legislative assembly shall be held in nineteen hundred and eleven.

Sec. 6. In addition to sections sixteen and thirty-six, heretofore granted to the territory of New Mexico, sections two and thirty-two in every township in said proposed state not otherwise appropriated at the date of the passage of this act are hereby granted to the said state for the support of common schools; and where sections two, sixteen, thirty-two, and thirty-six, or any parts thereof, are mineral, or have been sold, reserved, or otherwise appropriated or reserved by or under the authority of any act of congress, or are wanting or fractional in quantity, or where settlement thereon with a view to pre-emption or homestead, or improvement thereof with a view to desert-land entry has been made heretofore or hereafter, and before the survey thereof in the field, the provisions of sections twenty-two hundred and seventy-five and twenty-two hundred and seventy-six of the revised statutes are hereby made applicable thereto and to the selection of lands in lieu thereof to the same extent as if sections two and thirty-two, as well as sections sixteen and thirty-six, were mentioned therein: Provided, however, That the area of such indemnity selections on account of any fractional township shall not in any event exceed an area which, when added to the area of the above-named sections returned by the survey as in place, will equal four sections for fractional townships containing seventeen thousand two hundred and eighty acres or more, three sections for such townships containing eleven thousand five hundred and twenty acres or more, two sections for such townships containing five thousand seven hundred and sixty acres or more, nor one section for such township containing six hundred and forty acres or more: And provided further, That the grants of sections two, sixteen, thirty-two, and thirty-six to said state, within national forests now existing or proclaimed, shall not vest the title to said sections in said state until the part of said national forests embracing any of said sections is restored to the public domain; but said granted sections shall be administered as a part of said forests, and at the close of each fiscal year there shall be paid by the secretary of the treasury to the state, as income for its common school fund, such proportion of the gross proceeds of all the national forests within said state as the area of lands hereby granted to said state for school purposes which are situate within said forest reserves, whether surveyed or unsurveyed, and for which no indemnity has been selected, may bear to the total area of all the national forests within said state, the area of said sections when unsurveyed to be determined by the secretary of the interior, by protraction or otherwise, the amount necessary for such payments being appropriated and made available annually from any money in the treasury not otherwise appropriated.

Sec. 7. In lieu of the grant of land for purposes of internal improvements made to new states by the eighth section of the act of September fourth, eighteen hundred and forty-one, and in lieu of the swamp-land grant made by the act of September twenty-eighth, eighteen hundred and fifty, and section twenty-four hundred and seventy-nine of the revised statutes, and in lieu of the grant of thirty thousand acres for each senator and representative in congress, made by the act of July second, eighteen hundred and sixty-two, twelfth statutes at large, page five hundred and three, which grants are hereby declared not to extend to the said state, and in lieu of the grant of saline lands heretofore made to the Territory of New Mexico for university purposes by section three of the act of June twenty-first, eighteen hundred and ninety-eight, which is hereby repealed, except to the extent of such approved selections of such saline lands as may have been made by said territory prior to the passage of this act, the following grants of lands are hereby made, to wit:

For university purposes, two hundred thousand acres; for legislative, executive, and judicial public buildings heretofore erected in said territory or to be hereafter erected in the proposed state, and for the payment of the bonds heretofore or hereafter issued therefor, one hundred thousand acres; for insane asylums, one hundred thousand acres; for penitentiaries, one hundred thousand acres; for schools and asylums for the deaf, dumb, and the blind, one hundred thousand acres; for miners' hospitals for disabled miners, fifty thousand acres; for normal schools, two hundred thousand acres; for state charitable, penal, and reformatory institutions, one hundred thousand acres; for agricultural and mechanical colleges, one hundred and fifty thousand acres; and the national appropriation heretofore annually paid for the agricultural and mechanical college to said territory shall, until further order of congress, continue to be paid to said state for the use of said institution; for school of mines, one hundred and fifty thousand acres; for military institutes, one hundred thousand acres; and for the payment of the bonds and accrued interest thereon issued by Grant and Santa Fe counties, New Mexico, which said bonds were validated, approved, and confirmed by act of congress of January sixteenth, eighteen hundred and ninety-seven (twenty-ninth statutes, page four hundred and eighty-seven), one million acres: Provided, That if there shall remain any of the one million acres of land so granted, or of the proceeds of the sale or lease thereof, or rents, issues, or profits therefrom, after the payment of said debts, such remainder of lands and the proceeds of sales thereof shall be added to and become a part of the permanent school fund of said state, the income therefrom only to be used for the maintenance of the common schools of said state.

Sec. 8. The schools, colleges, and universities provided for in this act shall forever remain under the exclusive control of the said state, and no part of the proceeds arising from the sale or disposal of any lands granted herein for educational purposes shall be used for the support of any sectarian or denominational school, college, or university.

Sec. 9. Five per centum of the proceeds of sales of public lands lying within said state, which shall be sold by the United States subsequent to the admission of said state into the union, after deducting all the expenses incident to such sales, shall be paid to the said state to be used as a permanent inviolable fund, the interest of which only shall be expended for the support of the common schools within said state.

Sec. 10. It is hereby declared that all lands hereby granted, including those which, having been heretofore granted to the said territory, are hereby expressly transferred and confirmed to the said state, shall be by the said state held in trust, to be disposed of in whole or in part only in manner as herein provided and for the several objects specified in the respective granting and confirmatory provisions, and that the natural products and money proceeds of any of said lands shall be subject to the same trusts as the lands producing the same.

Disposition of any of said lands, or of any money or thing of value directly or indirectly derived therefrom, for any object other than that for which such particular lands, or the lands from which such money or thing of value shall have been derived, were granted or confirmed, or in any manner contrary to the provisions of this act, shall be deemed a breach of trust; Provided, however, That the state of New Mexico, through proper legislation, may provide for the payment, out of the income from the lands herein granted, which land may be included in a drainage district, of such assessments as have been duly and regularly established against any such lands in properly organized drainage districts under the general drainage laws of said state.

No mortgage or other encumbrance of the said lands, or any thereof, shall be valid in favor of any person or for any purpose or under any circumstances whatsoever. Said lands shall not be sold or leased, in whole or in part, except to the highest and best bidder at a public auction to be held at the county seat of a county wherein the lands to be affected, or the major portion thereof, shall lie, notice of which public auction shall first have been duly given by advertisement, which shall set forth the nature, time, and place of the transaction to be had, with a full description of the lands to be offered, and be published once each week for not less than ten successive weeks in a newspaper of general circulation published regularly at the state capital, and in that newspaper of like circulation which shall then be regularly published nearest to the location of such lands so offered; nor shall any sale or contract for the sale of any timber or other natural product of such lands be made, save at the place, in the manner, and after the notice by publication thus provided for sales and leases of the lands themselves: Provided, That nothing herein contained shall prevent said proposed state from leasing any of said lands referred to in this section for a term of five years or less without said advertisement herein required.

All lands, leaseholds, timber, and other products of land before being offered shall be appraised at their true value, and no sale or other disposal thereof shall be made for a consideration less than the value so ascertained, nor in any case less than the minimum price hereinafter fixed, nor upon credit unless accompanied by ample security, and the legal title shall not be deemed to have passed until the consideration shall have been paid.

Lands east of the line between ranges eighteen and nineteen east of the New Mexico principal meridian shall not be sold for less than five dollars per acre, and lands west of said line shall not be sold for less than three dollars per acre, and no lands which are or shall be susceptible of irrigation under any projects now or hereafter completed or adopted by the United States under legislation for the reclamation of lands, or under any other project for the reclamation of lands, shall be sold at less than twenty-five dollars per acre: Provided, That said state, at the request of the secretary of the interior, shall from time to time relinquish such of its lands to the United States as at any time are needed for irrigation works in connection with any such government project. And other lands in lieu thereof are hereby granted to said state, to be selected from lands of the character named and in the manner prescribed in section eleven of this act.

There is hereby reserved to the United States and exempted from the operation of any and all grants made or confirmed by this act to said proposed state all land actually or prospectively valuable for the development of water powers or power for hydroelectric use or transmission and which shall be ascertained and designated by the secretary of the interior within five years after the proclamation of the president declaring the admission of the state; and no lands so reserved and excepted shall be subject to any disposition whatsoever by said state, and any conveyance or transfer of such land by said state or any officer thereof shall be absolutely null and void within the period above named; and in lieu of the land so reserved to the United States and excepted from the operation of any of said grants, there be, and is hereby, granted to the proposed state an equal quantity of land to be selected from land of the character named and in the manner prescribed in section eleven of this act.

Every sale, lease, conveyance, or contract of or concerning any of the lands hereby granted or confirmed, or the use thereof or the natural products thereof, not made in substantial conformity with the provisions of this act shall be null and void, any provision of the constitution or laws of the said state to the contrary notwithstanding.

It shall be the duty of the attorney general of the United States to prosecute in the name of the United States and its courts such proceedings at law or in equity as may from time to time be necessary and appropriate to enforce the provisions hereof relative to the application and disposition of the said lands and the products thereof and the funds derived therefrom.

Nothing herein contained shall be taken as in limitation of the power of the state or of any citizen thereof to enforce the provisions of this act; Provided, That the secretary of the interior is hereby authorized in his discretion to accept on behalf of the United States, title to any land within the exterior boundaries of the national forests in the state of New Mexico, title to which is in the state of New Mexico, which the said state of New Mexico is willing to convey to the United States, and which shall be so conveyed by deed duly recorded and executed by the governor of said state and the state land commissioner, with the approval of the state land board of said state, and as to land granted to the said state of New Mexico for the support of common schools with the approval of the state superintendent of public instruction of said state, as to institutional grant lands with the approval of the governing body of the institution for whose benefit the lands so reconveyed were granted to said state, if, in the opinion of the secretary of agriculture, public interests will be benefited thereby and the lands are chiefly valuable for national forest purposes, and in exchange therefor, the secretary of the interior, in his discretion, may give not to exceed an equal value of unappropriated, ungranted, national forest or other government land belonging to the United States within the said state of New Mexico, as may be determined by the secretary of agriculture and be acceptable to the state as a fair compensation, consideration being given to any reservation which either the state or the United States may make of timber, mineral or easements.

Authority is hereby vested in the president temporarily to withdraw from disposition under the act of June 25, 1910 (thirty-sixth statutes at large, page 847), as amended by the act of August 24, 1912 (thirty-seventh statutes at large, page 497), lands proposed for selection by the state under the provisions of this act. (As amended April 1, 1926, 44 Stat. 228, ch. 96; June

15, 1926, 44 Stat. 746, ch. 590, 1; Aug. 28, 1957, 71 Stat. 457, P.L. 85-180.)

Sec. 11. All lands granted in quantity or as indemnity by this act shall be selected, under the direction and subject to the approval of the secretary of the interior, from the surveyed, unreserved, unappropriated, and nonmineral public lands of the United States within the limits of said state, by a commission composed of the governor, surveyor-general, or other officer exercising the functions of a surveyor-general, and the attorney general of the said state; and after its admission into the union said state may procure public lands of the United States within its boundaries to be surveyed with a view to satisfying any public land grants made to said state in the same manner prescribed for the procurement of such surveys by Washington, Idaho, and other states by the act of congress approved August eighteenth, eighteen hundred and ninety-four (twenty-eighth statutes at large, page three hundred and ninety-four), and the provisions of said act, in so far as they relate to such surveys and the preference right of selection, are hereby extended to the said state of New Mexico. The fees to be paid to the register and receiver for each final location or selection of one hundred and sixty acres made hereunder shall be one dollar.

Sec. 12. All grants of lands heretofore made by any act of congress to said territory, except to the extent modified or repealed by this act, are hereby ratified and confirmed to said state, subject to the provisions of this act: Provided, however, That nothing in this act contained shall, directly or indirectly, affect any litigation now pending and to which the United States is a party, or any right or claim therein asserted.

Sec. 13. The state, when admitted as aforesaid, shall constitute one judicial district, and the district court of said district shall be held at the capital of said state, and the said district shall, for judicial purposes, be attached to the eighth judicial circuit. There shall be appointed for said district one district judge, one United States attorney, and one United States marshal. The judge of said district shall receive a yearly salary the same as other similar judges of the United States, payable as provided for by law, and shall reside in the district to which he is appointed. There shall be appointed a clerk of said court, who shall keep his office at the capital of said state. The regular terms of said court shall be held on the first Monday in March and the first Monday in September of each year. The district court for said district, and the judges thereof shall possess the same powers and jurisdiction and perform the same duties required to be performed by the other district court and judges of the United States, and shall be governed by the same laws and regulations. The marshal, district attorney, and the clerks of the district court of said district, and all other officers and persons performing duties in the administration of justice therein, shall severally possess the powers and perform the duties lawfully possessed and required to be performed by similar officers in other districts of the United States, and shall, for the services they may perform, receive the fees and compensation now allowed by law to officers performing similar services for the United States in the Territory of New Mexico. (As amended March 4, 1921, 41 Stat. 1361, ch. 149.)

Sec. 14. All cases of appeal or writ of error and all other proceedings heretofore lawfully prosecuted and now pending in the supreme court of the United States or in the proper circuit court of appeals upon any record from the supreme court of said territory, and all cases of appeal or writ of error and all other proceedings heretofore lawfully prosecuted and now pending in the supreme court of the United States upon any record from a district court of said territory or in any matter of habeas corpus upon any return or order of a district judge thereof, and all and singular the cases aforesaid which, hereafter shall be so lawfully prosecuted and remain pending in the supreme court of the United States or in the proper circuit court of appeals, may be heard and determined by the supreme court of the United States or the proper circuit court of appeals, as the case may be. And the mandate of execution or of further proceedings shall be directed by the supreme court of the United States or the circuit court of appeals to the circuit or district court, hereby established within the said state, or to the supreme court of such state, as the nature of the case may require. And the circuit, district, and state courts herein named shall respectively be the successors of the supreme court and of the district courts of the said territory as to all such cases arising within the limits embraced within the jurisdiction of said courts, respectively, with full power to proceed with the same and award mesne or final process therein; and that from all judgments and decrees or other determinations of any court of the said territory, in any case begun prior to admission, the parties to such cause shall have the same right to prosecute appeals and writs of error to the supreme court of the United States or to the circuit court of appeals as they would have had by law prior to the admission of said state into the union.

Sec. 15. The said circuit or the said district court, as the case may be, shall have jurisdiction to hear and determine all trials, proceedings, and questions arising, or which may be raised, in any case or controversy pending in any of the courts other than the supreme court of the said territory at the date of its admission as a state, the case being such that, under the laws of the United States touching the jurisdictions of federal courts, it might properly have been begun in or (as a separable controversy or otherwise) removed to said circuit or said district court, had they been established when the litigation of such case or controversy was commenced. Should such case or controversy be such that, if begun within a state, it would have fallen within the exclusive original cognizance of a circuit or district court of the United States sitting therein, it shall be transferred to the one or the other of said courts sitting within said State of New Mexico, with due regard for the general provisions of law defining their respective jurisdictions; but should such case or controversy be by nature one of those which under such general jurisdictional provisions fall within the concurrent but not the exclusive jurisdiction of such courts, then such transfer may be had upon application of any party to such case or controversy, to be made as nearly as may be in the manner now provided for removal of cases from state to federal courts, and not later than sixty days after the lodgment of the record of such case or controversy in the proper court of the state, as herein provided. All cases and controversies pending at the admission of the state, and not transferable to the said circuit or district court under the foregoing provision, shall be heard and determined by the proper court of the state. All files, records, and proceedings relating to any such pending cases or controversies shall be transferred to such circuit, district, and state courts, respectively, in such wise and so authenticated or proven as such courts shall respectively, by rule direct, and upon transfer of any case or controversy, as herein provided, the same shall be proceeded with in due course of law; and no writ, action, indictment, information, cause, or proceeding pending in any court of the said territory at the time of its admission as a state shall abate or be deemed ineffective by reason of such admission, but the same shall be transferred and proceeded with in the proper circuit or district court of the United States, or state court, as the case may be: Provided, however, That all cases pending and undisposed of in the supreme court of the said territory at the time of the admission thereof as a state shall be transferred, together with the records thereof, to the highest appellate court of the state, and shall be heard and determined thereby, and appeal to and writ of error from the supreme court of the United States shall lie to review all such cases in accordance with the rules and principles applicable to the review by that tribunal of cases determined by state courts: Provided further, That all cases so pending in said territorial supreme court in which the United States is a party or which, if instituted within a state, would have fallen within the exclusive original cognizance of a circuit or district court of the United States, shall, with the records appertaining thereto, be transferred to the circuit court of appeals for the eighth circuit, and be there heard and decided; and any such case which, if finally decided by the supreme court of the territory, would have been in any manner reviewable by the supreme court of the United States, may in like manner and with like effect be so reviewed after final decision thereof by said circuit court of appeals. Transfers of all files and records from the said territorial supreme court to the highest appellate court of the state and to the said circuit court of appeals, shall be accomplished in such manner and under such proofs and authentications as the two last-mentioned courts shall respectively by rule prescribe.

All civil causes of action and all criminal offenses which shall have arisen or been committed prior to the admission of said territory as a state, but as to which no suit, action, or prosecution shall be pending at the date of such admission, shall be subject to prosecution in the courts of said state and the said circuit or district courts of the United States sitting therein, and to review in the appellate courts of such respective sovereignties in like manner and to the same extent as if said state had been created and such circuit, district, and state courts had been established prior to the accrual of such causes of action and the commission of such offenses; and in effectuation of this provision such of the said criminal offenses as shall have been committed against the laws of the said territory shall be tried and punished by the appropriate courts of the said state, and such as shall have been committed against the laws of the United States shall be tried and punished in the circuit or district courts of the United States.

All suits and actions brought by the United States in which said territory is named as a party defendant, which shall be pending in any court of said territory at the date of its admission hereunder, shall be transferred as herein provided; and the said state shall be substituted therein and become a party defendant thereto in lieu of said territory.

Sec. 16. The members of the legislature elected at the election hereinbefore provided for may assemble at Santa Fe, organize, and elect two senators of the United States in the manner now prescribed by the constitution and laws of the United States; and the governor and secretary of state of the proposed state shall certify the election of the senators and representatives in the manner required by law; and the senators and representatives so elected shall be entitled to be admitted to seats in congress and to all rights and privileges of senators and representatives of other states in the congress of the United States; and the officers of the state government formed in pursuance of said constitution, as provided by the constitutional convention, shall proceed to exercise all the functions of state officers; and all laws of said territory in force at the time of its admission into the union shall be in force in said state until changed by the legislature of said state, except as modified or changed by this act or by the constitution of the state; and the laws of the United States shall have the same force and effect within the said state as elsewhere within the United States.

Sec. 17. The sum of one hundred thousand dollars, or so much thereof as may be necessary, is hereby appropriated, out of any money in the treasury not otherwise appropriated, for defraying all and every kind and character of expense incident to the elections and convention provided for in this act; that is, the payment of the expenses of holding the election for members of the constitutional convention and the election for the ratification of the constitution, at the same rates that are paid for similar services under the territorial laws, and for the payment of the mileage for and salaries of members of the constitutional convention at the same rates that are paid to members of the said territorial legislature under national law, and for the payment of all proper and necessary expenses, officers, clerks, and messengers thereof, and printing and other expenses incident thereto: Provided, That any expense incurred in excess of said sum of one hundred thousand dollars shall be paid by said state. The said money shall be expended under the direction of the secretary of the interior, and shall be forwarded, to be locally expended in the present territory of New Mexico, through the secretary of said territory as may be necessary and proper, in the discretion of the secretary of the interior, in order to carry out the full intent and meaning of this act.

Sec. 18. All saline lands in the proposed State of New Mexico are hereby reserved from entry, location, selection, or settlement until such time as congress shall hereafter provide for their disposition.

16

Congressional Joint Resolution to Admit New Mexico and Arizona as States, 1911

Under the terms of the Enabling Act, New Mexico and Arizona prepared and ratified constitutions. The New Mexico Constitution was formally approved by President William H. Taft on February 24, 1911 and sent to the Congress for its approval. The Senate failed to act, but a joint resolution to admit New Mexico and Arizona was passed during a special session of Congress, only to be vetoed by Taft, who objected to provisions in the Arizona Constitution. Finally, a compromise measure was signed by Taft on August 21, 1911.

CONGRESSIONAL RESOLUTION
Joint Resolution to Admit the Territories of New Mexico and Arizona as States into the Union upon an Equal Footing with the Original States

(Joint Resolution of August 21, 1911, No. 8)

Section 1. The Territories of New Mexico and Arizona are hereby admitted into the union upon an equal footing with the original states, in accordance with the terms of an act entitled "An act to enable the people of New Mexico to form a constitution and state government and be admitted into the union on an equal footing with the original states; and to enable the people of Arizona to form a constitution and state government and be admitted into the union on an equal footing with the original states" commonly called the Enabling Act approved June twentieth, nineteen hundred and ten, and upon the terms and conditions hereinafter set forth. The admission herein provided for shall take effect upon the proclamation of the president of the United States, when the conditions explicitly set forth in this joint resolution shall have been complied with, which proclamation shall issue at the earliest practicable time after the results of the election herein provided for shall have been certified to the president, and also after evidence shall have been submitted to him of the compliance with the terms and conditions of this resolution.

The president is authorized and directed to certify the adoption of this resolution to the governor of each territory as soon as practicable after the adoption hereof, and each of said governors shall issue his proclamation for the holding of the first general election as provided for in the constitution of New Mexico heretofore adopted and the election ordinance numbered two adopted by the constitutional convention of Arizona, respectively, and for the submission to a vote of the electors of said territories of the amendments of the constitutions of said proposed states, respectively, herein set forth in accordance with the terms and conditions of this joint resolution. The results of said elections shall be certified to the president by the governor of each of said territories; and if the terms and conditions of this joint resolution shall have been complied with, the proclamation shall immediately issue by the president announcing the result of said elections so ascertained, and upon the issuance of said proclamation the proposed state or states so complying shall be deemed admitted by congress into the union upon an equal footing with the other states.

Sec. 2. The admission of New Mexico shall be subject to the terms and conditions of a joint resolution approved February sixteenth, nineteen hundred and eleven, and entitled "Joint resolution reaffirming the boundary line between Texas and the Territory of New Mexico."

Sec. 3. Before the proclamation of the president shall issue announcing the result of said election in New Mexico, and at the same time that the state election aforesaid is held, the electors of New Mexico shall vote upon the following proposed amendment of their state constitution as a condition precedent to the admission of said state, to wit:

"ARTICLE XIX of the constitution, as adopted by the electors of New Mexico at an election held on the twenty-first day of January, anno Domini nineteen hundred and eleven, be, and the same is hereby, amended so as to read as follows:

" 'ARTICLE XIX
" 'AMENDMENT

" 'Section 1. Any amendment or amendments to this constitution may be proposed in either house of the legislature at any regular session thereof; and if a majority of all members elected to each of the two houses voting separately shall vote in favor thereof, such proposed amendment or amendments shall be entered on their respective journals with the yeas and nays thereon.

" 'The secretary of state shall cause any such amendment or amendments to be published in at least one newspaper in every county of the state, where a newspaper is published once each week, for four consecutive weeks, in English and Spanish when newspapers in both of said languages are published in such counties, the last publication to be not more than two weeks prior to the election at which time said amendment or amendments shall be submitted to the electors of the state for their approval or rejection; and the said amendment or amendments shall be voted upon at the next regular election held in said state after the adjournment of the legislature proposing such amendment or amendments, or at such special election to be held not less than six months after the adjournment of said legislature, at such time as said legislature may by law provide. If the same be ratified by a majority of the electors voting thereon such amendment or amendments shall become part of this constitution. If two or more amendments are proposed, they shall be so submitted as to enable the electors to vote on each of them separately: Provided, That no amendment shall apply to or affect the provisions of sections one and three of Article VII hereof, on elective franchise, and sections eight and ten of Article XII hereof, on education, unless it be proposed by a vote of three-fourths of the members elected to each house and be ratified by a vote of the people of this state in an election at which at least three-fourths of the electors voting in the whole state and at least two-thirds of those voting in each county in the state shall vote for such amendment.

" 'Sec. 2. Whenever, during the first twenty-five years after the adoption of this constitution, the legislature, by a three-fourths vote of the members elected to each house, or, after the expiration of said period of twenty-five years, by a two-thirds vote of the members elected to each house, shall deem it necessary to call a convention to revise or amend this constitution, they shall submit the question of calling such convention to the electors at the next general election, and if a majority of all the electors voting on such question at said election in the state shall vote in favor of calling a convention the legislature shall, at the next session, provide by law for calling the same. Such conventions shall consist of at least as many delegates as there are members of the house of representatives. The constitution adopted by such convention shall have no validity until it has been submitted to and ratified by the people.

" 'Sec. 3. If this constitution be in any way so amended as to allow laws to be enacted by direct vote of the electors the laws which may be so enacted shall be only such as might be enacted by the legislature under the provisions of this constitution.

" 'Sec. 4. When the United States shall consent thereto, the legislature, by a majority vote of the members in each house, may submit to the people the question of amending any provision of Article XXI of this constitution on compact with the United States to the extent allowed by the act of congress permitting the same, and if a majority of the qualified electors who vote upon any such amendment shall vote in favor thereof the said article shall be thereby amended accordingly.

" 'Sec. 5. The provisions of section one of this article shall not be changed, altered, or abrogated in any manner except through a general convention called to revise this constitution as herein provided.' "

Sec. 4. The probate clerks of the several counties of New Mexico shall provide separate ballots for the use of the electors at said first state election for the purpose of voting upon said amendment. Said separate ballots shall be printed on paper of a blue tint, so that they may be readily distinguished from the white ballots provided for the election of county and state officers. Said separate ballots shall be delivered only to the election officers authorized by law to receive and have the custody of the ballot boxes for use at said election and shall be delivered by them only to the individual voter and only one ballot to each elector at the time he offers to vote at the said general election, and shall have the initials of two election officers of opposite political parties written by them upon the back thereof. Said separate ballot shall not be marked either for or against the said amendment at the time it is handed to the elector by the election officer, and if the elector desires to vote upon said amendment, the ballot must be marked by the voter, unless he shall request one of the election officers to mark the same for him, in which case such election officer so called upon shall mark said ballot as such voter shall request. Any elector receiving such ballot shall return the same before leaving the polls to one of the election judges, who shall immediately deposit the same in the ballot box whether such ballot be marked or not. No ballots on said amendment except those so handed to said electors and so initialed shall be deposited in the ballot box or counted or canvassed. Said separate ballots shall have printed thereon the proposed amendment in both the English and the Spanish language. There shall be placed on said ballots two blank squares with dimensions of one-half an inch and opposite one of said squares shall be printed in both the English and the Spanish language the words ''For constitutional amendment,'' and opposite the other blank square shall be printed in both the English and the Spanish language the words ''Against constitutional amendment.''

Any elector desiring to vote for said amendment shall mark his ballot with a cross in the blank square opposite the words ''For constitutional amendment,'' or cause the same to be so marked by an election officer as aforesaid, and any elector desiring to vote against said amendment shall mark his ballot with a cross in the blank square opposite the words ''Against constitutional amendment,'' or cause the same to be so marked by an election officer as aforesaid.

Sec. 5. Said ballots shall be counted and canvassed by said election officers, and the returns of said election upon said amendment shall be made by said election officers direct to the secretary of the Territory of New Mexico at Santa Fe, who, with the governor and chief justice of said territory, shall constitute a canvassing board; and they, or any two of them, shall meet at said City of Santa Fe on the third Monday after said election and shall canvass the same. If a majority of the legal votes cast at said election upon said amendment shall be in favor thereof, the said canvassing board shall forthwith certify said result to the governor of the territory, together with the statement of votes cast upon the question of the ratification or rejection of said amendment; whereupon the governor of said territory shall by proclamation declare the said amendment a part of the constitution of the proposed State of New Mexico, and thereupon the same shall become and be a part of said constitution; but if the same shall fail of such majority, then Article XIX of the constitution of New Mexico as adopted on January twenty-first, nineteen hundred and eleven, shall remain a part of said constitution.

Except as herein otherwise provided, said election upon this amendment shall be in all respects subject to the election laws of New Mexico now in force.

Sec. 6. The fifth clause of section two of ''An act to enable the people of New Mexico to form a constitution and state government and be admitted into the union on an equal footing with the original states; and to enable the people of Arizona to form a constitution and be admitted into the union on an equal footing with the original states,'' approved June twentieth, anno Domini nineteen hundred and ten, be, and the same is hereby, amended so as to read as follows:

''Fifth. That said state shall never enact any law restricting or abridging the right of suffrage on account of race, color, or previous condition of servitude.''

17

President Taft's Proclamation Admitting New Mexico as a State, 1912

On January 6, 1912, some sixty-six years after Kearny occupied New Mexico and almost sixty-four years after the Treaty of Guadalupe Hidalgo, President Taft issued a proclamation admitting New Mexico into the Union. Turning to witnesses, he said, "Well, it is all over. I am glad to give you life. I hope you will be healthy."

PROCLAMATION ADMITTING NEW MEXICO AS A STATE INTO THE UNION
(January 6, 1912)

WHEREAS the congress of the United States did by an act approved on the twentieth day of June, one thousand nine hundred and ten, authorize the people of the Territory of New Mexico to form a Constitution and state government, and provide for the admission of such state into the Union on an equal footing with the original states upon certain conditions in said act specified:

AND WHEREAS said people did adopt a Constitution and ask admission into the Union:

AND WHEREAS the congress of the United States did pass a joint resolution, which was approved on the twenty-first day of August, one thousand nine hundred and eleven, for the admission of the state of New Mexico into the Union, which resolution required that the electors of New Mexico should vote upon an amendment of their state Constitution, which was proposed and set forth at length in said resolution of congress, as a condition precedent to the admission of said state, and that they should so vote at the same time that the first general election as provided for in the said Constitution should be held:

AND WHEREAS it appears from information laid before me that said first general state election was held on the seventh day of November, one thousand nine hundred and eleven, and that the returns of said election upon said amendment were made and canvassed as in section five of said resolution of congress provided:

AND WHEREAS the governor of New Mexico has certified to me the result of said election upon said amendment and of the said general election:

AND WHEREAS the conditions imposed by the said act of congress approved on the twentieth day of June, one thousand nine hundred and ten, and by the said joint resolution of congress have been fully complied with:

NOW, THEREFORE, I, William Howard Taft, President of the United States of America, do, in accordance with the provisions of the act of congress and the joint resolution of congress herein named, declare and proclaim the fact that the fundamental conditions imposed by congress on the state of New Mexico to entitle that state to admission have been ratified and accepted, and that the admission of the state into the Union on an equal footing with the other states is now complete.

IN TESTIMONY WHEREOF, I have hereunto set my hand and caused the seal of the United States to be affixed.

DONE at the City of Washington this sixth day of January, in the year of our Lord one thousand nine hundred and twelve and of the Independence of the United States of America the one hundred and thirty-sixth.

WM H TAFT

By the President:
P C KNOX
Secretary of State.

18

Governor Lindsey's Proclamation at Start of World War I, 1917

On April 2, 1917, after a long period of crises and negotiations, President Woodrow Wilson delivered his war message to Congress, and on April 6, the United States declared war on Germany. Twenty days later Governor W.E. Lindsey called a special session of the State Legislature to enact special legislation to assist the war effort.

BY THE GOVERNOR OF THE STATE OF NEW MEXICO.
A PROCLAMATION.

WHEREAS, the Congress has declared that a state of war exists between the United States of America and the Imperial German government; and,

WHEREAS, in order to prosecute the said war, it is declared to be the purpose of the general government to recruit from among the citizens of our country, approximately two millions of men and equip, train and maintain them in war time efficiency, besides the further necessary enlistments for the immediate full equipment of the navy; thus calling from among the body of our people a large fraction of our producers; and,

WHEREAS, during thirty-three months, seventeen nations and sixty-five peoples have been engaged in the most destructive warfare that the world has yet seen; thus calling from among the productive industries millions of the world's ablest producers, so that, coupled with untoward crop seasons in many countries, an unprecedented food shortage exists; and,

WHEREAS, the State of New Mexico produces annually less than fifty per centum of the food product consumed by her people,

Therefore, necessity demands that a special session of the Third State Legislature of New Mexico be called:

NOW, THEREFORE, I, W.E. LINDSEY, GOVERNOR OF THE STATE OF NEW MEXICO, by virtue of the powers vested in me as such, do hereby call the Third State Legislature of the State of New Mexico, to meet in the Capitol Building, in the City of Santa Fe, in the State of New Mexico, at twelve o'clock noon, Tuesday, May 1st, 1917, for the purpose of enacting such legislation as will enable the State of New Mexico to:

1. Provide for its own defense and to assist the United States in the prosecution of the war.

2. Provide for and regulate the production, conservation, distribution and marketing of foods.

3. Enact such laws as will provide the necessary resources to meet the expenses arising out of the emergencies of the war.

4. Accept the provisions of the "Smith-Hughes" Congressional Act of February 23rd, 1917.

5. Pay the expense of the session hereby called.

And for the accomplishment of each and all of these ends, to make all such appropriations of money as shall be necessary and required.

IN WITNESS WHEREOF I HAVE HEREUNTO SET MY HAND AND CAUSED THE GREAT SEAL OF THE STATE OF NEW MEXICO TO BE AFFIXED.

Done at the CITY OF SANTA FE, this 26th Day of April, 1917.

W.E. LINDSEY

By the Governor:
ANTONIO LUCERO
Secretary of State.

19

Governor Miles's Proclamation at Start of World War II, 1941

On December 8, 1941, the day after the Japanese attack on Pearl Harbor, the United States declared war on Japan, and on December 11, Germany and Italy declared war on the United States. Governor John Miles declared a state of emergency on December 8.

A PROCLAMATION BY THE GOVERNOR

WHEREAS, troops of a foreign nation have, without just cause, fired upon American troops, civilians, and property on American soil, and,

WHEREAS, the Congress of the United States has declared a state of war to exist and,

WHEREAS, New Mexico is one of the forty-eight sovereign states of the Union,

NOW, THEREFORE, I, JOHN E. MILES, GOVERNOR OF THE STATE OF NEW MEXICO, do hereby declare a full emergency to exist and urge that all citizens of this state cooperate to the fullest extent with municipal, county, state, and Federal governments, and in full harmony, strive in our common cause until our armed forces have time to exact just retribution from our treacherous, despicable, and infamous foe.

Done at the Executive Office,
this 8th day of December, 1941.
WITNESS MY HAND AND THE GREAT
SEAL OF THE STATE OF NEW MEXICO.
JOHN E. MILES
Governor

Attest:
JESSIE M. GONZALES
Secretary of State

20

Constitution of the State of New Mexico, as Adopted in 1911 and Amended through 1974

The constitutional convention of 1910 consisted of seventy-one Republicans and twenty-nine Democrats. Among the members were such well-known individuals as Thomas B. Catron, Holm Bursum, Albert Fall, Solomon Luna, and Harvey Fergusson. The proceedings of the convention were somewhat unusual in that no verbatim record was made. Although Fergusson and others opposed the Constitution as too conservative, it was ratified by a vote of 31,742 to 13, 399.

CONSTITUTION
of the
STATE OF NEW MEXICO

As Adopted January 21, 1911
and as Subsequently Amended by the People in General and Special
Elections, 1912 through 1974

PREAMBLE

We, the people of New Mexico, grateful to Almighty God for the blessings of liberty, in order to secure the advantages of a state government, do ordain and establish this Constitution.

ARTICLE I
Name and Boundaries

The name of this state is New Mexico, and its boundaries are as follows:

Beginning at the point where the thirty-seventh parallel of north latitude intersects the one hundred and third meridian west from Greenwich; thence along said one hundred and third meridian to the thirty-second parallel of north latitude; thence along said thirty-second parallel to the Rio Grande, also known as the Rio Bravo del Norte, as it existed on the ninth day of September, one thousand eight hundred and fifty; thence, following the main channel of said river, as it existed on the ninth day of September, one thousand eight hundred and fifty, to the parallel of thirty-one degrees forty-seven minutes north latitude; thence west one hundred miles to a point; thence south to the parallel of thirty-one degrees twenty minutes north latitude; thence along said parallel of thirty-one degrees twenty minutes, to the thirty-second meridian of longitude west from Washington; thence along said thirty-second meridian to the thirty-seventh parallel of north latitude; thence along said thirty-seventh parallel to the point of beginning.

ARTICLE II
Bill of Rights

Section 1. The State of New Mexico is an inseparable part of the Federal Union, and the Constitution of the United States is the supreme law of the land.

Sec. 2. All political power is vested in and derived from the people, all government of right originates with the people, is founded upon their will and is instituted solely for their good.

Sec. 3. The people of the state have the sole and exclusive right to govern themselves as a free, sovereign and independent state.

Sec. 4. All persons are born equally free, and have certain natural, inherent and inalienable rights, among which are the rights of enjoying and defending life and liberty, of acquiring, possessing and protecting property, and of seeking and obtaining safety and happiness.

Sec. 5. The rights, privileges and immunities, civil, political and religious guaranteed to the people of New Mexico by the Treaty of Guadalupe Hidalgo shall be preserved inviolate.

Sec. 6. No law shall abridge the right of the citizen to keep and bear arms for security and defense, for lawful hunting and recreational use and for other lawful purposes, but nothing herein shall be held to permit the carrying of concealed weapons. (As amended November 2, 1971.)

Sec. 7. The privilege of the writ of habeas corpus shall never be suspended, unless, in case of rebellion or invasion, the public safety requires it.

Sec. 8. All elections shall be free and open, and no power, civil or military, shall at any time interfere to prevent the free exercise of the right of suffrage.

Sec. 9. The military shall always be in strict subordination to the civil power; no soldier shall in time of peace be quartered in any house without the consent of the owner, nor in time of war except in the manner prescribed by law.

Sec. 10. The people shall be secure in their persons, papers, homes and effects, from unreasonable searches and seizures, and no warrant to search any place, or seize any person or thing, shall issue without describing the place to be searched, or the persons or things to be seized, nor without a written showing of probable cause, supported by oath or affirmation.

Sec. 11. Every man shall be free to worship God according to the dictates of his own conscience, and no person shall ever be molested or denied any civil or political right or privilege on account of his religious opinion or mode of religious worship. No person shall be required to attend any place of worship or support any religious sect or denomination; nor shall any preference be given by law to any religious denomination or mode of worship.

Sec. 12. The right of trial by jury as it has heretofore existed shall be secured to all and remain inviolate. In all cases triable in courts inferior to the district court the jury may consist of six. The legislature may provide that verdicts in civil cases may be rendered by less than a unanimous vote of the jury.

Sec. 13. All persons shall be bailable by sufficient sureties, except for capital offenses when the proof is evident or the presumption great. Excessive bail shall not be required, nor excessive fines imposed, nor cruel and unusual punishment inflicted.

Sec. 14. No person shall be held to answer for a capital, felonious or infamous crime unless on a presentment or indictment of a grand jury or information filed by a district attorney or attorney general or their deputies, except in cases arising in the militia when in actual service in time of war or public danger. No person shall be so held on information without having had a preliminary examination before an examining magistrate, or having waived such preliminary examination.

A grand jury shall be composed of such number, not less than twelve, as may be prescribed by law. Citizens only, residing in the county for which a grand jury may be convened and qualified as prescribed by law, may serve on a grand jury. Concurrence necessary for the finding of an indictment by a grand jury shall be prescribed by law; provided, such concurrence shall never be by less than a majority of those who compose a grand jury, and, provided, at least eight must concur in finding an indictment when a grand jury is composed of twelve in number. Until otherwise prescribed by law a grand jury shall be composed of twelve in number of which eight must concur in finding an indictment. A grand jury shall be convened upon order of a judge of a court empowered to try and determine cases of capital, felonious or infamous crimes at such times as to him shall be deemed necessary, or a grand jury shall be ordered to convene by such judge upon the filing of a petition therefor signed by not less than seventy-five resident taxpayers of the county, or a grand jury may be convened in any additional manner as may be prescribed by law.

In all criminal prosecutions, the accused shall have the right to appear and defend himself in person, and by counsel; to demand the nature and cause of the accusation; to be confronted with the witnesses against him; to have the charge and testimony interpreted to him in a language that he understands; to have compulsory process to compel the attendance of necessary witnesses in his behalf, and a speedy public trial by an impartial jury of the county or district in which the offense is alleged to have been committed. (As amended November 4, 1924, effective January 1, 1925.)

Sec. 15. No person shall be compelled to testify against himself in a criminal proceeding, nor shall any person be twice put in jeopardy for the same offense; and when the indictment, information or affidavit upon which any person is convicted charges different offenses or different degrees of the same offense and a new trial is granted the accused, he may not again be tried for an offense or degree of the offense greater than the one of which he was convicted.

Sec. 16. Treason against the state shall consist only in levying war against it, adhering to its enemies, or giving them aid and comfort. No person shall be convicted of treason unless on the testimony of two witnesses to the same overt act, or on confession in open court.

Sec. 17. Every person may freely speak, write and publish his sentiments on all subjects, being responsible for the abuse of that right; and no law shall be passed to restrain or abridge the liberty of speech or of the press. In all criminal prosecutions for libels, the truth may be given in evidence to the jury; and if it shall appear to the jury that the matter charged as libelous is true and was published with good motives and for justifiable ends, the party shall be acquitted.

Sec. 18. No person shall be deprived of life, liberty or property without due process of law; nor shall any person be denied equal protection of the laws. Equality of rights under law shall not be denied on account of the sex of any person. The effective date of this amendment shall be July 1, 1973. (As amended November 7, 1972.)

Sec. 19. No ex post facto law, bill of attainder, nor law impairing the obligation of contracts shall be enacted by the legislature.

Sec. 20. Private property shall not be taken or damaged for public use without just compensation.

Sec. 21. No person shall be imprisoned for debt in any civil action.

Sec. 22. Until otherwise provided by law no alien, ineligible to citizenship under the laws of the United States, or corporation, copartnership or association, a majority of the stock or interest in which is owned or held by such aliens, shall acquire title, leasehold or other interest in or to real estate in New Mexico. (As amended September 20, 1921.)

Sec. 23. The enumeration in this Constitution of certain rights shall not be construed to deny, impair or disparage others retained by the people.

ARTICLE III
Distribution of Powers

Section 1. The powers of the government of this state are divided into three distinct departments, the legislative, executive and judicial, and no person or collection of persons charged with the exercise of powers properly belonging to one of these departments, shall exercise any powers properly belonging to either of the others, except as in this Constitution otherwise expressly directed or permitted.

ARTICLE IV
Legislative Department

Section 1. The legislative power shall be vested in a senate and house of representatives which shall be designated the legislature of the state of New Mexico, and shall hold its sessions at the seat of government.

The people reserve the power to disapprove, suspend and annul any law enacted by the legislature, except general appropriation laws; laws providing for the preservation of the public peace, health or safety; for the payment of the public debt or interest thereon, or the creation or funding of the same, except as in this Constitution otherwise provided; for the maintenance of the public schools or state institutions, and local or special laws. Petitions disapproving any law other than those above excepted, enacted at the last preceding session of the legislature, shall be filed with the secretary of state not less than four months prior to the next general election. Such petitions shall be signed by not less than ten per centum of the qualified electors of each of three-fourths of the counties and in the aggregate by not less than ten per centum of the qualified electors of the state, as shown by the total number of votes cast at the last preceding general election. The question of the approval or rejection of such law shall be submitted by the secretary of state to the electorate at the next general election; and if a majority of the legal votes cast thereon, and not less than forty per centum of the total number of legal votes cast at such general election, be cast for the rejection of such law, it shall be annulled and thereby repealed with the same effect as if the legislature had then repealed it, and such repeal shall revive any law repealed by the act so annulled; otherwise, it shall remain in force unless subsequently repealed by the legislature. If such petition or petitions be signed by not less than twenty-five per centum of the qualified electors under each of the foregoing conditions, and be filed with the secretary of state within ninety days after the adjournment of the session of the legislature at which such law was enacted, the operation thereof shall be thereupon suspended and the question of its approval or rejection shall be likewise submitted to a vote at the next ensuing general election. If a majority of the votes cast thereon and not less than forty per centum of the total number of votes cast at such general election be cast for its rejection, it shall be thereby annulled; otherwise, it shall go into effect upon publication of the certificate of the secretary of state declaring the result of the vote thereon. It shall be a felony for any person to sign any such petition with any name other than his own, or to sign his name more than once for the same measure, or to sign such petition when he is not a qualified elector in the county specified in such petition; provided, that nothing herein shall be construed to prohibit the writing thereon of the name of any person who cannot write, and who signs the same with his mark. The legislature shall enact laws necessary for the effective exercise of the power hereby reserved.

Sec. 2. In addition to the powers herein enumerated, the legislature shall have all powers necessary to the legislature of a free state, including the power to enact reasonable and appropriate laws to guarantee the continuity and effective operation of state and local government by providing emergency procedure for use only during periods of disaster emergency. A disaster emergency is defined as a period when damage or injury to persons or property in this state, caused by enemy attack, is of such magnitude that a state of martial law is declared to exist in the state, and a disaster emergency is declared by the chief executive officer of the United States and the chief executive officer of this state, and the legislature has not declared by joint resolution that the disaster emergency is ended. Upon the declaration of a disaster emergency the chief executive of the state shall within seven [7] days call a special session of the legislature which shall remain in continuous session during the disaster emergency, and may recess from time to time for [not] more than three [3] days. (As amended November 8, 1960.)

Sec. 3. a. Senators shall not be less than twenty-five [25] years of age and representatives not less than twenty-one [21] years of age at the time of their election. If any senator or representative permanently removes his residence from or maintains no residence in the county from which he was elected, then he shall be deemed to have resigned and his successor shall be selected as provided in section 4 of this article. No person shall be eligible to serve in the legislature who, at the time of qualifying, holds any office of trust or profit with the state, county or national governments, except notaries public and officers of the militia who receive no salary.

b. [The senate shall consist of one [1] senator from each county of the state. In the event the number of counties is hereafter increased or decreased, the number of senators shall be increased or decreased accordingly at the next election thereafter at which members of the senate are to be elected.]

c. Until changed as provided herein, the house of representatives shall consist of sixty-six [66] members, composed of at least one [1] member elected from each county of the state, Provided that the county of Bernalillo shall elect a total of nine [9] members; the counties of Chaves, Dona Ana, Eddy, Lea, McKinley, Rio Arriba, San Juan, San Miguel and Santa Fe shall elect a total of three [3] members each; and the counties of Colfax, Curry, Grant, Otero, Quay, Roosevelt, Taos and Valencia shall elect a total of two [2] members each.

d. For the purpose only of selection in each county entitled to elect more than one [1] member of the house of representatives, there shall be designated by the officer issuing the election proclamation as many places, consecutively numbered, as there shall be representatives to be elected in such county, and only one [1] member of the house of representatives shall be elected for each place designated. No county shall be geographically divided for the purpose of designating places in the election of such members of the house of representatives. Each candidate shall designate, upon filing his petition, the position number for which he is a candidate, and the county clerk shall so designate him upon the ballot.

e. Upon the creation of any new county, it shall be entitled to elect one [1] member of the house of representatives at the next general election following its creation.

f. Once following publication of the official report of each federal decennial census hereafter conducted, the legislature may by statute reapportion among the various counties the number of members of the house of representatives to be elected from each county, Provided that each county shall be entitled to elect at least one [1] member of the house of representatives, and that no member of the house of representatives shall represent or be elected by the voters of more than one [1] county. (As amended September 20, 1949 and September 20, 1955.)

Sec. 4. [Members of the legislature shall be elected as follows: Those senators from Bernalillo, Chaves, Curry, DeBaca, Grant, Lea, Lincoln, Luna, Sandoval, San Juan, San Miguel, Socorro, Taos, Torrance, Union and Valencia counties for a term of six [6] years starting January 1, 1961, and after serving such terms shall be elected for a term of four [4] years thereafter; those senators from all other counties for the terms of four [4] years, and members of the house of representatives for a term of two [2] years. They shall be elected on the day provided by law for holding the general election of state officers or representatives in Congress. If a vacancy occurs in the office of senator or member of the house of representatives, for any reason, the county commissioners of the county wherein the vacancy occurs shall fill such vacancy by appointment.]

Such legislative appointments as provided in this section shall be for a term ending on December 31, subsequent to the next succeeding general election. (As amended September 15, 1953 and November 8, 1960.)

Sec. 5. A. Each regular session of the legislature shall begin annually at 12:00 noon on the third Tuesday of January. Every regular session of the legislature convening during an odd-numbered year shall remain in session not to exceed sixty [60] days, and every regular session of the legislature convening during an even-numbered year shall remain in session not to exceed thirty [30] days. No special session of the legislature shall exceed thirty [30] days.

B. Every regular session of the legislature convening during an even-numbered year shall consider only the following:

(1) budgets, appropriations and revenue bills;

(2) bills drawn pursuant to special messages of the governor; and

(3) bills of the last previous regular session vetoed by the governor.

(As amended November 5, 1940, November 5, 1946 and November 3, 1964.)

Sec. 6. Special sessions of the legislature may be called by the governor, but no business shall be transacted except such as relates to the objects specified in this proclamation. Provided, however, that when three-fifths of the members elected to the house of representatives and three-fifths of the members elected to the senate shall have certified to the governor of the state of New Mexico that in their opinion an emergency exists in the affairs of the state of New Mexico, it shall thereupon be the duty of said governor and mandatory upon him, within five (5) days from the receipt of such certificate or certificates, to convene said legislature in extraordinary session for all purposes; and in the event said governor shall, within said time, Sundays excluded, fail or refuse to convene said legislature as aforesaid, then and in that event said legislature may convene its3lf in extraordinary session, as if convened in regular session, for all purposes, provided that such extraordinary self-convened session shall be limited to a period of thirty [30] days, unless at the expiration of said period, there shall be pending an impeachment trial of some officer of the state government, in which event the legislature shall be authorized to remain in session until such trial shall have been completed. (As amended November 2, 1948.)

Sec. 7. Each house shall be the judge of the election and qualifications of its own members. A majority of either house shall constitute a quorum to do business, but a less number may effect a temporary organization, adjourn from day to day, and compel the attendance of absent members.

Sec. 8. The senate shall be called to order in the hall of the senate by the lieutenant-governor. The senate shall elect a president pro tempore who shall preside in the absence of the lieutenant-governor and shall serve until the next session of the legislature. The house of representatives shall be called to order in the hall of said house by the secretary of state. He shall preside until the election of a speaker, who shall be the member receiving the highest number of votes for that office.

Sec. 9. The legislature shall select its own officers and employees and fix their compensation. Each house shall have one chaplain, one chief clerk, and one sergeant-at-arms; and there shall be one assistant chief clerk and one assistant sergeant-at-arms for each house; and each house may employ such enrolling clerks, reading clerks, stenographers, janitors and such subordinate employees in addition to those enumerated, as they may reasonably require and their compensation shall be fixed by the said legislature at the beginning of each session. (As amended November 2, 1948.)

Sec. 10. Each member of the legislature shall receive:

A. as per diem expense the sum of not more than forty dollars for each day's attendance during each session, as provided by law, and ten cents for each mile traveled in going to and returning from the seat of government by the usual traveled route, once each session as defined by Section 5, Article IV, of this Constitution;

B. per diem expense and mileage at the same rate as provided in Subsection A for service at meetings required by legislative committees established by the legislature to meet in the interim between sessions; and

C. no other compensation, perquisite or allowance. (As amended November 7, 1944; September 15, 1953 and November 2, 1971.)

Sec. 11. Each house may determine the rules of its procedure, punish its members or others for contempt or disorderly behavior in its presence, and protect its members against violence; and may, with the concurrence of two-thirds of its members, expel a member, but not a second time for the same act. Punishment for contempt or disorderly behavior or by expulsion shall not be a bar to criminal prosecution. (As amended September 15, 1953.)

Sec. 12. All sessions of each house shall be public. Each house shall keep a journal of its proceedings and the yeas and nays on any questions shall, at the request of one-fifth of the members present, be entered thereon. The original thereof shall be filed with the secretary of state at the close of the session, and shall be printed and published under his authority.

Sec. 13. Members of the legislature shall, in all cases except treason, felony and breach of the peace, be privileged from arrest during their attendance at the sessions of their respective houses, and on going to and returning from the same. And they shall not be questioned in any other place for any speech or debate or for any vote cast in either house.

Sec. 14. Neither house shall, without the consent of the other, adjourn for more than three days, Sundays excepted; nor to any other place than that where the two houses are sitting; and on the day of the final adjournment they shall adjourn at twelve o'clock noon.

Sec. 15. No law shall be passed except by bill, and no bill shall be so altered or amended on its passage through either house as to change its original purpose. The enacting clause of all bills shall be: "Be it enacted by the legislature of the state of New Mexico." Any bill may originate in either house. No bill, except bills to provide for the public peace, health and safety, and the codification or revision of the laws, shall become a law unless it has been printed, and read three different times in each house, not more than two of which readings shall be on the same day, and the third of which shall be in full.

Sec. 16. The subject of every bill shall be clearly expressed in its title, and no bill embracing more than one subject shall be passed except general appropriation bills and bills for the codification or revision of the laws; but if any subject is embraced in any act which is not expressed in its title, only so much of the act as is not so expressed shall be void. General appropriation bills shall embrace nothing but appropriations for the expense of the executive, legislative and judiciary departments, interest, sinking fund, payments on the public debt, public schools, and other expenses required by existing laws; but if any such bill contain any other matter, only so much thereof as is hereby forbidden to be placed therein shall be void. All other appropriations shall be made by separate bills.

Sec. 17. No bill shall be passed except by a vote of a majority of the members present in each house, nor unless on its final passage a vote be taken by yeas and nays, and entered on the journal.

Sec. 18. No law shall be revised or amended, or the provisions thereof extended by reference to its title only; but each section thereof as revised, amended or extended shall be set out in full.

Notwithstanding the foregoing or any other provision of this Constitution, the legislature, in any law imposing a tax or taxes, may define the amount on, in respect to or by which such tax or taxes are imposed or measured, by reference to any provision of the laws of the United States as the same may be or become effective at any time or from time to time, and may prescribe exceptions or modifications to any such provision. (As amended November 3, 1964.)

Sec. 19. Time limitation on the introduction of bills at any session of the legislature shall be established by law. (As amended November 8, 1932 and November 8, 1960.)

Sec. 20. Immediately after the passage of any bill or resolution, it shall be enrolled and engrossed, and read publicly in full in each house, and thereupon shall be signed by the presiding officers of each house in open session, and the fact of such reading and signing shall be entered on the journal. No interlineation or erasure in a signed bill, shall be effective, unless certified thereon in express terms by the presiding officer of each house quoting the words interlined or erased, nor unless the fact of the making of such interlineation or erasure be publicly announced in each house and entered on the journal.

Sec. 21. Any person who shall, without lawful authority, materially change or alter, or make away with, any bill pending in or passed by the legislature, shall be deemed guilty of a felony and upon conviction thereof shall be punished by imprisonment in the penitentiary for not less than one year nor more than five years.

Sec. 22. Every bill passed by the legislature shall, before it becomes a law, be presented to the governor for approval. If he approves, he shall sign it, and deposit it with the secretary of state; otherwise, he shall return it to the house in which it originated, with his objections, which shall be entered at large upon the journal; and such bill shall not become a law unless thereafter approved by two-thirds of the members present and voting in each house by yea or nay vote entered upon its journal. Any bill not returned by the governor within three days, Sundays excepted, after being presented to him, shall become a law, whether signed by him or not, unless the legislature by adjournment prevent such return. Every bill presented to the governor during the last three days of the session shall be approved by him within twenty days after the adjournment and shall be by him immediately deposited with the secretary of state. Unless so approved and signed by him such bill shall not become a law. The governor may in like manner approve or disapprove any part or parts, item or items, of any bill appropriating money, and such parts or items approved shall become a law, and such as are disapproved shall be void unless passed over his veto, as herein provided. (As amended September 15, 1953.)

Sec. 23. Laws shall go into effect ninety days after the adjournment of the legislature enacting them, except general appropriation laws, which shall go into effect immediately upon their passage and approval. Any act necessary for the preservation of the public peace, health or safety, shall take effect immediately upon its passage and approval, provided it be passed by two-thirds vote of each house and such necessity be stated in a separate section.

Sec. 24. The legislature shall not pass local or special laws in any of the following cases: Regulating county, precinct or district affairs; the jurisdiction and duties of justices of the peace, police magistrates and constables; the practice in courts of justice; the rate of interest on money; the punishment for crimes and misdemeanors; the assessment or collection of taxes or extending the time of collection thereof; the summoning and impaneling of jurors; the management of public schools; the sale or mortgaging of real estate of minors or others under disability; the change of venue in civil or criminal cases. Nor in the following cases: Granting divorces; laying out, opening, altering or working roads or highways, except as to state roads extending into more than one county, and military roads; vacating roads, town plats, streets, alleys or public grounds; locating or changing county seats, or changing county lines, except in creating new counties; incorporating cities, towns or villages, or changing or amending the charter of any city, town or village; the opening or conducting of any election or designating the place of voting; declaring any person of age; chartering or licensing ferries, toll bridges, toll roads, banks, insurance companies, or loan and trust companies; remitting fines, penalties, forfeitures or taxes; or refunding money paid into the state treasury, or relinquishing, extending or extinguishing, in whole or in part, any indebtedness or liability of any person or corporation, to the state or any municipality therein; creating, increasing or decreasing fees, percentages or allowances of public officers; changing the laws of descent; granting to any corporation, association or individual the right to lay down railroad tracks or any special or exclusive privilege, immunity or franchise, or amending existing charters for such purpose; changing the rules of evidence in any trial or inquiry; the limitation of actions; giving effect to any informal or invalid deed, will or other instrument; exempting property from taxation; restoring to citizenship any person convicted of an infamous crime; the adoption or legitimizing of children; changing the name of persons or places; and the creation, extension or impairment of liens. In every other case where a general law can be made applicable, no special law shall be enacted.

Sec. 25. No law shall be enacted legalizing the unauthorized or invalid act of any officer, remitting any fine, penalty or judgment against any officer, or validating any illegal use of public funds.

Sec. 26. The legislature shall not grant to any corporation or person, any rights, franchises, privileges, immunities or exemptions, which shall not, upon the same terms and under like conditions, inure equally to all persons or corporations; no exclusive right, franchise, privilege or immunity shall be granted by the legislature or any municipality in this state.

Sec. 27. No law shall be enacted giving any extra compensation to any public officer, servant, agent or contractor after services are rendered or contract made; nor shall the compensation of any officer be increased or diminished during his term of office, except as otherwise provided in this Constitution.

Sec. 28. No member of the legislature shall, during the term for which he was elected, be appointed to any civil office in the state, nor shall he within one year thereafter be appointed to any civil office created, or the emoluments of which were increased during such term; nor shall any member of the legislature during the term for which he was elected nor within one year thereafter, be interested directly or indirectly in any contract with the state or any municipality thereof, which was authorized by any law passed during such term.

Sec. 29. No law authorizing indebtedness shall be enacted which does not provide for levying a tax sufficient to pay the interest, and for the payment at maturity of the principal.

Sec. 30. Except interest or other payments on the public debt, money shall be paid out of the treasury only upon appropriations made by the legislature. No money shall be paid therefrom except upon warrant drawn by the proper officer. Every law making an appropriation shall distinctly specify the sum appropriated and the object to which it is to be applied.

Sec. 31. No appropriation shall be made for charitable, educational or other benevolent purposes to any person, corporation, association, institution or community, not under the absolute control of the state, but the legislature may, in its discretion, make appropriations for the charitable institutions and hospitals, for the maintenance of which annual appropriations were made by the legislative assembly of nineteen hundred and nine.

Sec. 32. No obligation or liability of any person, association or corporation held or owned by or owing to the state, or any municipal corporation therein, shall ever be exchanged, transferred, remitted, released, postponed, or in any way diminished by the legislature, nor shall any such obligation or liability be extinguished except by the payment thereof into the proper treasury, or by proper proceeding in court. Provided that the obligations created by Special Session Laws 1955, Chapter 5 running to the state or any of its agencies, remaining unpaid on the effective date of this amendment are void. (As amended November 4, 1958.)

Sec. 33. No person shall be exempt from prosecution and punishment for any crime or offenses against any law of this state by reason of the subsequent repeal of such law.

Sec. 34. No act of the legislature shall affect the right or remedy of either party, or change the rules of evidence or procedure, in any pending case.

Sec. 35. The sole power of impeachment shall be vested in the house of representatives, and a concurrence of a majority of all the members elected shall be necessary to the proper exercise thereof. All impeachments shall be tried by the senate. When sitting for that purpose the senators shall be under oath or affirmation to do justice according to the law and the evidence. When the governor or lieutenant-governor is on trial, the chief justice of the Supreme Court shall preside. No person shall be convicted without the concurrence of two-thirds of the senators elected.

Sec. 36. All state officers and judges of the district court shall be liable to impeachment for crimes, misdemeanors and malfeasance in office, but judgment in such cases shall not extend further than removal from office and disqualification to hold any office of honor, trust or profit, or to vote under the laws of this state; but such officer or judge, whether convicted or acquitted shall, nevertheless, be liable to prosecution, trial, judgment, punishment or civil action, according to law. No officer shall exercise any powers or duties of his office after notice of his impeachment is served upon him until he is acquitted.

Sec. 37. It shall not be lawful for a member of the legislature to use a pass, or to purchase or receive transportation over any railroad upon terms not open to the general public; and the violation of this section shall work a forfeiture of the office.

Sec. 38. The legislature shall enact laws to prevent trusts, monopolies and combinations in restraint of trade.

Sec. 39. Any member of the legislature who shall vote or use his influence for or against any matter pending in either house in consideration of any money, thing of value, or promise thereof, shall be deemed guilty of bribery; and any member of the legislature or other person who shall directly or indirectly offer, give or promise any money, thing of value, privilege or personal advantage, to any member of the legislature to influence him to vote or work for or against any matter pending in either house; or any member of the legislature who shall solicit from any person or corporation any money, thing of value or personal advantage for his vote or influence as such member shall be deemed guilty of solicitation of bribery.

Sec. 40. Any person convicted of any of the offenses mentioned in sections thirty-seven and thirty-nine hereof, shall be deemed guilty of a felony and upon conviction shall be punished by fine of not more than one thousand dollars or by imprisonment in the penitentiary for not less than one nor more than five years.

Sec. 41. Any person may be compelled to testify in any lawful investigation or judicial proceeding against another charged with bribery or solicitation of bribery as defined herein, and shall not be permitted to withhold his testimony on the ground that it might incriminate or subject him to public infamy; but such testimony shall not be used against him in any judicial proceeding against him except for perjury in giving such testimony.

ARTICLE V
Executive Department

Section 1. The executive department shall consist of a governor, lieutenant-governor, secretary of state, state auditor, state treasurer, attorney general and commissioner of public lands, who shall, unless otherwise provided in the Constitution of New Mexico, be elected for the term of four years beginning on the first day of January next after their election. The governor and lieutenant-governor shall be elected jointly by the casting by each voter of a single vote applicable to both offices.

Such officers shall, after having served one term, be ineligible to hold any state office until one full term has intervened, except that the lieutenant-governor may be eligible to hold the office of the governor.

The officers of the executive department, except the lieutenant-governor, shall during their terms of office, reside and keep the public records, books, papers and seals of office at the seat of government.

Upon the adoption of this amendment by the people, the terms provided for in this section shall apply to those officers elected at the general election in 1970 and all state executive officers elected thereafter. Provided, no person who has been elected to a state executive office prior to the adoption of this amendment for two successive terms shall again be eligible to hold the same office unless one full term has intervened; provided, further, the commissioner of public lands, the attorney general and state treasurer, elected to a two-year term in 1968, are eligible to hold the office of commissioner of public lands, the attorney general or the state treasurer, respectively, for one four-year term following his present term, but thereafter shall not again be eligible to hold the office of commissioner of public lands, attorney general or state treasurer, respectively, until one full term has intervened. (As amended November 3, 1970.)

Sec. 2. The returns of every election for state officers shall be sealed up and transmitted to the secretary of state, who, with the governor and chief justice, shall constitute the state canvassing board which shall canvass and declare the result of the election. The joint candidates having the highest number of votes cast for governor and lieutenant-governor and the person having the highest number of votes for any other office, as shown by said returns, shall be declared duly elected. If two or more have an equal, and the highest, number of votes for the same office or offices, one of them, or any two for whom joint votes were cast for governor and lieutenant-governor respectively, shall be chosen therefor by the legislature on joint ballot. (As amended November 6, 1962.)

Sec. 3. No person shall be eligible to any office specified in section one, hereof, unless he be a citizen of the United States, at least thirty years of age, nor unless he shall have resided continuously in New Mexico for five years next preceding his election; nor to the office of attorney general, unless he be a licensed attorney of the Supreme Court of New Mexico in good standing; nor to the office of superintendent of public instruction unless he be a trained and experienced educator.

Sec. 4. The supreme executive power of the state shall be vested in the governor, who shall take care that the laws be faithfully executed. He shall be commander in chief of the military forces of the state, except when they are called into the service of the United States. He shall have power to call out the militia to preserve the public peace, execute the laws, suppress insurrection and repel invasion.

Sec. 5. The governor shall nominate, and, by and with the consent of the senate, appoint all officers whose appointment or election is not otherwise provided for, and may remove any officer appointed by him for incompetency, neglect of duty or malfeasance in office. Should a vacancy occur in any state office, except lieutenant-governor and member of the legislature, the governor shall fill such office by appointment, and such appointee shall hold office until the next general election, when his successor shall be chosen for the unexpired term.

Sec. 6. Subject to such regulations as may be prescribed by law, the governor shall have power to grant reprieves and pardons, after conviction for all offenses except treason and in cases of impeachment.

Sec. 7. If at the time fixed for the beginning of the term of the governor, the governor-elect shall have died, the lieutenant governor-elect shall become governor. If a governor shall not have been chosen before the time fixed for the beginning of his term, or if the governor-elect shall have failed to qualify, then the lieutenant governor-elect shall act as governor until a governor shall have qualified; and the legislature may by law provide for the case wherein neither a governor-elect nor a lieutenant governor-elect shall have qualified, declaring who shall then act as governor, or the manner in which one who is to act shall be selected, and such person shall act accordingly until a governor or lieutenant-governor shall have qualified.

If after the governor-elect has qualified a vacancy occurs in the office of governor, the lieutenant-governor shall succeed to that office, and to all the powers, duties and emoluments thereof, provided he has by that time qualified for the office of lieutenant-governor. In case the governor is absent from the state, or is for any reason unable to perform his duties, the lieutenant-governor shall act as governor, with all the powers, duties and emoluments of that office until such disability be removed. In case there is no lieutenant-governor, or in case he is for any reason unable to perform the duties of governor, then the secretary of state shall perform the duties of governor, and, in case there is no secretary of state, then the president pro tempore of the senate, or in case there is no president pro tempore of the senate, or he is for any reason unable to perform the duties of governor, then the speaker of the house shall succeed to the office of governor, or act as governor as hereinbefore provided. (As amended November 2, 1948.)

Sec. 8. The lieutenant-governor shall be president of the senate, but shall vote only when the senate is equally divided.

Sec. 9. Each officer of the executive department and of the public institutions of the state shall keep an account of all moneys received by him and make reports thereof to the governor under oath, annually, and at such other times as the governor may require, and shall, at least thirty days preceding each regular session of the legislature, make a full and complete report to the governor, who shall transmit the same to the legislature.

Sec. 10. There shall be a state seal which shall be called the "Great Seal of the State of New Mexico," and shall be kept by the secretary of state.

Sec. 11. All commissions shall issue in the name of the state, be signed by the governor and attested by the secretary of state, who shall affix the state seal thereto.

Sec. 12. The annual compensation to be paid to the officers mentioned in section one of this article shall be as follows: Governor, five thousand dollars; secretary of state, three thousand dollars; state auditor, three thousand dollars; state treasurer, three thousand dollars; attorney general, four thousand dollars; superintendent of public instruction, three thousand dollars, and commissioner of public lands, three thousand dollars; which compensation shall be paid to the respective officers in equal quarterly payments.

The lieutenant-governor shall receive ten dollars per diem while acting as presiding officer of the senate, and mileage at the same rate as a state senator.

The compensation herein fixed shall be full payment for all services rendered by said officers and they shall receive no other fees or compensation whatsoever.

The compensation of any of said officers may be increased or decreased by law after the expiration of ten years from the date of the admission of New Mexico as a state.

Sec. 13. All district, county, precinct and municipal officers, shall be residents of the political subdivisions for which they are elected or appointed. The legislature is authorized to enact laws permitting division of counties of this state into county commission districts. The legislature may in its discretion provide that elective county commissioners reside in their respective county commission districts. (As amended November 8, 1960.)

Sec. 14. There is created a "state highway commission." The members of the state highway commission shall be appointed, shall have such power and shall perform such duties as may be provided by law. Notwithstanding the provisions of Article 5, Section 5, of the Constitution of New Mexico, state highway commissioners shall only be removed as provided by law. (As repealed and re-enacted November 7, 1967.)

ARTICLE VI
Judicial Department

Section 1. The judicial power of the state shall be vested in the senate when sitting as a court of impeachment, a Supreme Court, a court of appeals, district courts; probate courts, magistrate courts and such other courts inferior to the district courts as may be established by law from time to time in any district, county or municipality of the state. (As amended September 28, 1965 and November 8, 1966.)

Sec. 2. Appeals from a judgment of the district court imposing a sentence of death or life imprisonment shall be taken directly to the Supreme Court. In all other cases, criminal and civil, the Supreme Court shall exercise appellate jurisdiction as may be provided by law; provided that an aggrieved party shall have an absolute right to one appeal. (As amended September 28, 1965.)

Sec. 3. The Supreme Court shall have original jurisdiction in quo warranto and mandamus against all state officers, boards and commissions, and shall have a superintending control over all inferior courts; it shall also have power to issue writs of mandamus, error, prohibition, habeas corpus, certiorari, injunction and all other writs necessary or proper for the complete exercise of its jurisdiction and to hear and determine the same. Such writs may be issued by direction of the court, or by any justice thereof. Each justice shall have power to issue writs of habeas corpus upon petition by or on behalf of a person held in actual custody, and to make such writs returnable before himself or before the Supreme Court, or before any of the district courts or any judge thereof.

Sec. 4. The Supreme Court of the state shall consist of three justices, who shall be elected at the general election for representatives in Congress for a term of eight years.

At the first election for state officers after the adoption of this Constitution, there shall be elected three justices of the Supreme Court, who shall immediately qualify and classify themselves by lot, so that one of them shall hold office until four years, one until six years, and one until eight years, from and after the first day of January, nineteen hundred and thirteen. A certificate of such classification shall be filed in the office of the secretary of state. Until otherwise provided by law, the justice who has the shortest term to serve shall be the chief justice and shall preside at all sessions of the court; and in his absence the justice who has the next shortest term to serve shall preside; but no justice appointed or elected to fill a vacancy shall be a chief justice.

Sec. 5. A majority of the justices of the Supreme Court shall be necessary to constitute a quorum for the transaction of business, and a majority of the justices must concur in any judgment of the court.

Sec. 6. When a justice of the Supreme Court shall be interested in any case, or be absent, or incapacitated, the remaining justices of the court may, in their discretion, call in any district judge of the state to act as a justice of the court.

Sec. 7. The Supreme Court shall hold one term each year, commencing on the second Wednesday in January, and shall be at all times in session at the seat of government; provided, that the court may, from time to time, take such recess as in its judgment may be proper.

Sec. 8. No person shall be qualified to hold the office of justice of the Supreme Court unless he be at least thirty years old, learned in the law, and shall have been in the actual practice of law and resided in this state or the territory of New Mexico, for at least three years. Any person whose time of service upon the bench of any district court of this state or the territory of New Mexico, added to the time he may have practiced law, as aforesaid, shall be equal to three years, shall be qualified without having practiced for the full three years.

Sec. 9. The Supreme Court may appoint and remove at pleasure its reporter, bailiff, clerk and such other officers and assistants as may be prescribed by law.

Sec. 10. After the publication of the census of the United States in the year nineteen hundred and twenty, the legislature shall have power to increase the number of justices of the Supreme Court to five; provided, however, that no more than two of said justices shall be elected at one time, except to fill a vacancy.

Sec. 11. The justices of the Supreme Court shall each receive such salary as may hereafter be fixed by law. (As amended September 15, 1953.)

Sec. 12. The state shall be divided into eight judicial districts and a judge shall be chosen for each district by the qualified electors thereof at the election for representatives in Congress. The terms of office of the district judges shall be six years.

Sec. 13. The district court shall have original jurisdiction in all matters and causes not excepted in this Constitution, and such jurisdiction of special cases and proceedings as may be conferred by law, and appellate jurisdiction of all cases originating in inferior courts and tribunals in their respective districts, and supervisory control over the same. The district courts, or any judge thereof, shall have power to issue writs of habeas corpus, mandamus, injunction, quo warranto, certiorari, prohibition, and all other writs, remedial or otherwise in the exercise of their jurisdiction; provided, that no such writs shall issue directed to judges or courts of equal or superior jurisdiction. The district courts shall also have the power of naturalization in accordance with the laws of the United States. Until otherwise provided by law, at least two terms of the district court shall be held annually in each county, at the county seat.

Sec. 14. The qualifications of the district judges shall be the same as those of justices of the Supreme Court. Each district judge shall reside in the district for which he was elected.

Sec. 15. Any district judge may hold district court in any county at the request of the judge of such district.

Whenever the public business may require, the chief justice of the Supreme Court shall designate any district judge of the state, or any justice of the Supreme Court when no district judge may be available within a reasonable time, to hold court in any district, and two or more judges may sit in any district or county separately at the same time. If any judge shall be disqualified from hearing any cause in the district, the parties to such cause, or their attorneys of record, may select some member of the bar to hear and determine said cause, and act as judge pro tempore therein. (As amended November 8, 1938.)

Sec. 16. The legislature may increase the number of district judges in any judicial district, and they shall be elected as other district judges. At its first session after the publication of the census of the United States in the year nineteen hundred and twenty, and at the first session after each United States census thereafter, the legislature may rearrange the districts of the state, increase the number thereof, and make provision for a district judge for any additional district.

Sec. 17. The legislature shall provide by law for the compensation of the judges of the district court. (As amended September 15, 1953.)

Sec. 18. No justice, judge or magistrate of any court shall, except by consent of all parties, sit in any cause in which either of the parties are related to him by affinity or consanguinity within the degree of first cousin, or in which he was counsel, or in the trial of which he presided in any inferior court, or in which he has an interest. (As amended November 8, 1966.)

Sec. 19. No judge of the Supreme or district courts shall be nominated or elected to any other than a judicial office in this state.

Sec. 20. All writs and processes shall issue, and all prosecution shall be conducted in the name of ''The State of New Mexico.''

Sec. 21. Justices of the Supreme Court, in the state, and district judges and magistrates, in their respective jurisdictions, shall be conservators of the peace. District judges and other judges or magistrates designated by law may hold preliminary examinations in criminal cases. (As amended November 8, 1966.)

Sec. 22. Until otherwise provided by law, a county clerk shall be elected in each county who shall, in the county for which he is elected perform all the duties now performed by the clerks of the district courts and clerks of the probate courts.

Sec. 23. A probate court is hereby established for each county, which shall be a court of record, and, until otherwise provided by law, shall have the same jurisdiction as heretofore exercised by the probate courts of New Mexico and shall also have jurisdiction to determine heirship with respect to real property in all proceedings for the administration of decedents' estates. The legislature shall have power from time to time to confer upon the probate court in any county in this state jurisdiction to determine heirship in all probate proceedings, and shall have power also from time to time to confer upon the probate court in any county in this state general civil jurisdiction co-extensive with the county; provided, however, that such court shall not have jurisdiction in civil cases in which the matter in controversy shall exceed in value three thousand dollars ($3,000.00) exclusive of interest and cost; nor in any action for malicious prosecution, slander and libel; nor in any action against officers for misconduct in office; nor in any action for the specific performance of contracts for the sale of real estate; nor in any action for the possession of land; nor in any matter wherein the title or boundaries of land may be in dispute or drawn in question, except as title to real property may be affected by the determination of heirship; nor to grant writs of injunction, habeas corpus or extraordinary writs. Jurisdiction may be conferred upon the judges of said court to act as examining and committing magistrates in criminal cases, and upon said courts for the trial of misdemeanors in which the punishment cannot be imprisonment in the penitentiary, or in which the fine cannot be in excess of one thousand dollars ($1,000). A jury for the trial of such cases shall consist of six men. The legislature shall prescribe the qualifications and fix the compensation of probate judges. (As amended September 20, 1949.)

Sec. 24. There shall be a district attorney for each judicial district, who shall be learned in the law, and who shall have been a resident of New Mexico for three years next prior to his election, shall be the law officer of the state and of the counties within his district, shall be elected for a term of four years, and shall perform such duties and receive such salary as may be prescribed by law.

The legislature shall have the power to provide for the election of additional district attorneys in any judicial district and to designate the counties therein for which the district attorneys shall serve; but no district attorney shall be elected for any district of which he is not a resident.

Sec. 25. The state shall be divided into eight judicial districts, as follows:
First District. The counties of Santa Fe, Rio Arriba and San Juan.
Second District. The counties of Bernalillo, McKinley and Sandoval.
Third District. The counties of Dona Ana, Otero, Lincoln and Torrance.
Fourth District. The counties of San Miguel, Mora and Guadalupe.
Fifth District. The counties of Eddy, Chaves, Roosevelt and Curry.
Sixth District. The counties of Grant and Luna.
Seventh District. The counties of Socorro, Valencia and Sierra.
Eighth District. The counties of Taos, Colfax, Union and Quay.

In case of the creation of new counties the legislature shall have power to attach them to any contiguous district for judicial purposes.

Sec. 26. The legislature shall establish a magistrate court to exercise limited original jurisdiction as may be provided by law. The magistrate court shall be composed of such districts and elective magistrates as may be provided by law. Magistrates shall be qualified electors of, and reside in, their respective districts, and the legislature shall prescribe other qualifications. Magistrates shall receive compensation as may be provided by law, which compensation shall not be diminished during their term of office. (As repealed and re-enacted November 8, 1966.)

Sec. 27. Appeals shall be allowed in all cases from the final judgments and decisions of the probate courts and other inferior courts to the district courts, and in all such appeals, trial shall be had de novo unless otherwise provided by law. (As amended November 8, 1966.)

Sec. 28. The court of appeals shall consist of not less than three [3] judges whose qualifications shall be the same as those of justices of the Supreme Court and whose compensation and election for terms of eight [8] years shall be as provided by law, except that an initial term may be prescribed by law for less than eight [8] years to provide maximum continuity.

A vacancy in the office of judge of the court of appeals shall be filled by appointment of the governor for a period provided by law.

Three [3] judges of the court of appeals shall constitute a quorum for the transaction of business, and a majority of those participating must concur in any judgment of the court.

When necessary, the chief justice of the Supreme Court may designate any justice of the Supreme Court, or any district judge of the state, to act as a judge of the court of appeals, and he may designate any judge of the court of appeals to hold court in any district, or to act as a justice of the Supreme Court. (As added September 28, 1965.)

Sec. 29. The court of appeals shall have no original jurisdiction. It may be authorized by law to review directly decisions of administrative agencies of the state, and it may be authorized by rules of the Supreme Court to issue all writs necessary or appropriate in aid of its appellate jurisdiction. In all other cases, it shall exercise appellate jurisdiction as may be provided by law. (As added September 28, 1965.)

Sec. 30. All fees collected by the judicial department shall be paid into the state treasury as may be provided by law and no justice, judge or magistrate of any court shall retain any fees as compensation or otherwise. (As added November 8, 1966.)

Sec. 31. Justices of the peace shall be abolished not later than five [5] years from the effective date of this amendment and may, within this period, be abolished by law, and magistrate courts vested with appropriate jurisdiction. Until so abolished, justices of the peace shall be continued under existing laws. (As added November 8, 1966.)

Sec. 32. There is created the "judicial standards commission," consisting of two justices or judges and two lawyers selected as may be provided by law to serve for terms of four years, and five citizens, none of whom is a justice, judge or magistrate of any court or licensed to practice law in this state, who shall be appointed by the governor for five-year staggered terms as may be provided by law. If a position on the commission becomes vacant for any reason, the successor shall be selected by the original appointing authority in the same manner as the original appointment was made and shall serve for the remainder of the term vacated. No act of the commission is valid unless concurred in by a majority of its members. The commission shall select one of the members appointed by the governor to serve as chairman.

In accordance with this section, any justice, judge or magistrate of any court may be disciplined or removed for willful misconduct in office or willful and persistent failure to perform his duties or habitual intemperance, or he may be retired for disability seriously interfering with the performance of his duties which is, or is likely to become, of a permanent character. The commission may, after investigation it deems necessary, order a hearing to be held before it concerning the discipline, removal or retirement of a justice, judge or magistrate, or the commission may appoint three masters who are justices or judges of courts of record to hear and take evidence in the matter and to report their findings to the commission. After hearing or after considering the record and the findings and report of the masters, if the commission finds good cause, it shall recommend to the Supreme Court the discipline, removal or retirement of the justice, judge or magistrate.

The Supreme Court shall review the record of the proceedings on the law and facts and may permit the introduction of additional evidence, and it shall order the discipline, removal or retirement as it finds just and proper or wholly reject the recommendation. Upon an order for his retirement, any justice, judge or magistrate participating in a statutory retirement program shall be retired with the same rights as if he had retired pursuant to the retirement program. Upon an order for removal, the justice, judge or magistrate shall thereby be removed from office, and his salary shall cease from the date of the order.

All papers filed with the commission or its masters, and proceedings before the commission or its masters, are confidential. The filing of papers and giving of testimony before the commission or its masters is privileged in any action for defamation, except that the record filed by the commission in the Supreme Court continues privileged but, upon its filing, loses its confidential character, and a writing which was privileged prior to its filing with the commission or its masters does not lose its privilege by the filing. The commission shall promulgate regulations establishing procedures for hearings under this section. No justice or judge who is a member of the commission or Supreme Court shall participate in any proceeding involving his own discipline, removal or retirement.

This section is alternative to, and cumulative with, the removal of justices, judges and magistrates by impeachment and the original superintending control of the Supreme Court. (As added November 7, 1967.)

ARTICLE VII
Elective Franchise

Section 1. Every citizen of the United States, who is over the age of twenty-one years, and has resided in New Mexico twelve months, in the county ninety days, and in the precinct in which he offers to vote thirty days, next preceding the election, except idiots, insane persons, and persons convicted of a felonious or infamous crime unless restored to political rights, shall be qualified to vote at all elections for public officers. The legislature may enact laws providing for absentee voting by qualified electors. All school elections shall be held at different times from other elections.

The legislature shall have the power to require the registration of the qualified electors as a requisite for voting, and shall regulate the manner, time and places of voting. The legislature shall enact such laws as will secure the secrecy of the ballot, the purity of elections, and guard against the abuse of elective franchise. Not more than two members of the board of registration, and not more than two judges of election shall belong to the same political party at the time of their appointment. (As amended November 7, 1967.)

Sec. 2. A. Every citizen of the United States who is a legal resident of the state and is a qualified elector therein, shall be qualified to hold any elective public office except as otherwise provided in this Constitution.

B. The legislature may provide by law for such qualifications and standards as may be necessary for holding an appointive position by any public officer or employee.

C. The right to hold public office in New Mexico shall not be denied or abridged on account of sex, and wherever the masculine gender is used in this Constitution, in defining the qualifications for specific offices, it shall be construed to include the feminine gender. The payment of public road poll tax, school poll tax or service on juries shall not be made a prerequisite to the right of a person to vote or hold office. (As amended November 6, 1973.)

Sec. 3. The right of any citizen of the state to vote, hold office, or sit upon juries, shall never be restricted, abridged or impaired on account of religion, race, language or color, or inability to speak, read or write the English or Spanish languages except as may be otherwise provided in this Constitution; and the provisions of this section and of section one of this article shall never be amended except upon a vote of the people of this state in an election at which at least three-fourths of the electors voting in the whole state, and at least two-thirds of those voting in each county of the state, shall vote for such amendment.

Sec. 4. No person shall be deemed to have acquired or lost residence by reason of his presence or absence while employed in the service of the United States or of the state, nor while a student at any school.

Sec. 5. All elections shall be by ballot, and the person who receives the highest number of votes for any office, except in the case of the offices of governor and lieutenant governor, shall be declared elected thereto. The joint candidates receiving the highest number of votes for the offices of governor and lieutenant governor shall be declared elected to those offices. (As amended November 6, 1962.)

ARTICLE VIII
Taxation and Revenue

Section 1. Taxes levied upon tangible property shall be in proportion to the value thereof, and taxes shall be equal and uniform upon subjects of taxation of the same class. Different methods may be provided by law to determine value of different kinds of property, but the percentage of value against which tax rates are assessed shall not exceed thirty-three and one-third per cent. (As amended November 3, 1914 and November 2, 1971.)

Sec. 2. Taxes levied upon real or personal property for state revenue shall not exceed four mills annually on each dollar of the assessed valuation thereof except for the support of the educational, penal and charitable institutions of the state, payment of the state debt and interest thereon; and the total annual tax levy upon such property for all state purposes exclusive of necessary levies for the state debt shall not exceed ten mills; Provided, however, that taxes levied upon real or personal tangible property for all purposes, except special levies on specific classes of property and except necessary levies for public debt, shall not exceed twenty mills annually on each dollar of the assessed valuation thereof, but laws may be passed authorizing additional taxes to be levied outside of such limitation when approved by at least a majority of the qualified electors of the taxing district who paid a property tax therein during the preceding year voting on such proposition. (As amended November 3, 1914; September 19, 1933 and November 7, 1967.)

Sec. 3. The property of the United States, the state and all counties, towns, cities and school districts, and other municipal corporations, public libraries, community ditches and all laterals thereof, all church property not used for commercial purposes, all property used for educational or charitable purposes, all cemeteries not used or held for private or corporate profit, and all bonds of the state of New Mexico, and of the counties, municipalities and districts thereof shall be exempt from taxation.

Provided, however, that any property acquired by public libraries, community ditches and all laterals thereof, property acquired by churches, property acquired and used for educational or charitable purposes, and property acquired by cemeteries not used or held for private or corporate profit, and property acquired by the Indian service, and property acquired by

the United States government or by the state of New Mexico by outright purchase or trade, where such property was, prior to such transfer, subject to the lien of any tax or assessment for the principal or interest of any bonded indebtedness shall not be exempt from such lien, nor from the payment of such taxes or assessments.

Exemptions of personal property from ad valorem taxation may be provided by law if approved by a three-fourths majority vote of all the members elected to each house of the legislature. (As amended November 2, 1971.)

Sec. 4. Any public officer making any profit out of public moneys or using the same for any purpose not authorized by law, shall be deemed guilty of a felony and shall be punished as provided by law and shall be disqualified to hold public office. All public moneys not invested in interest-bearing securities shall be deposited in national banks in this state, in banks or trust companies incorporated under the laws of the state, or in federal savings and loan associations in this state, or in savings and loan associations incorporated under the laws of this state whose deposits are insured by an agency of the United States, and the interest derived therefrom shall be applied in the manner prescribed by law. The conditions of such deposits shall be provided by law. (As amended November 3, 1914 and November 7, 1967.)

Sec. 5. The legislature may exempt from taxation property of each head of the family to the amount of two hundred dollars ($200) and the property, including the community or joint property of husband and wife, of every honorably discharged member of the armed forces of the United States who served in such armed forces during any period in which they were or are engaged in armed conflict under orders of the president of the United States, and the widow or widower of every such honorably discharged member of the armed forces of the United States, in the sum of two thousand dollars ($2,000). Provided, that in every case where exemption is claimed on the ground of the claimant's having served with the armed forces of the United States as aforesaid, the burden of proving actual and bona fide ownership of such property upon which exemption is claimed, shall be upon the claimant. (As amended November 6, 1973.)

Sec. 6. Lands held in large tracts shall not be assessed for taxation at any lower value per acre then [than] lands of the same character or quality and similarly situated, held in smaller tracts. The plowing of land shall not be considered as adding value thereto for the purpose of taxation. (As amended November 3, 1914.)

Sec. 7. No execution shall issue upon any judgment rendered against the board of county commissioners of any county, or against any incorporated city, town or village, school district or board of education; or against any officer of any county, incorporated city, town or village, school district or board of education, upon any judgment recovered against him in his official capacity and for which the county, incorporated city, town or village, school district or board of education, is liable, but the same shall be paid out of the proceeds of a tax levy as other liabilities of counties, incorporated cities, towns or villages, school districts or boards of education, and when so collected shall be paid by the county treasurer to the judgment creditor. (As amended November 3, 1914.)

Sec. 8. Personal property which is moving in interstate commerce through or over the state of New Mexico, or which was consigned to a warehouse, public or private, or factory within New Mexico from outside the state for storage in transit to a final destination outside the state of New Mexico, manufacturing, processing or fabricating while in transit to a final destination, whether specified when transportation begins or afterwards, which destination is also outside the state, shall be deemed not to have acquired a situs in New Mexico for purposes of taxation and shall be exempt from taxation. Such property shall not be deprived of such exemption because while in the warehouse the property is assembled, bound, joined, processed, disassembled, divided, cut, broken in bulk, relabeled or repackaged. (As added November 6, 1973.)

Sec. 9. No tax or assessment of any kind shall be levied by any political subdivision whose enabling legislation does not provide for an elected governing authority. This section does not prohibit the levying or collection of a tax or special assessment by an initial appointed governing authority where the appointed governing authority will be replaced by an elected one within six years of the date the appointed authority takes office. The provisions of this section shall not be effective until July 1, 1976. (As amended November 5, 1974.)

ARTICLE IX
State, County and Municipal Indebtedness

Section 1. The state hereby assumes the debts and liabilities of the territory of New Mexico, and the debts of the counties thereof, which were valid and subsisting on June twentieth, nineteen hundred and ten, and pledges its faith and credit for the payment thereof. The legislature shall, at its first session, provide for the payment or refunding thereof by the issue and sale of bonds, or otherwise.

Sec. 2. No county shall be required to pay any portion of the debt of any other county so assumed by the state, and the bonds of Grant and Santa Fe Counties which were validated, approved and confirmed by Act of Congress of January sixteenth, eighteen hundred and ninety-seven, shall be paid as hereinafter provided.

Sec. 3. The bonds authorized by law to provide for the payment of such indebtedness shall be issued in three series, as follows:

Series A. To provide for the payment of such debts and liabilities of the territory of New Mexico.

Series B. To provide for the payment of such debts of said counties.

Series C. To provide for the payment of the bonds and accured interest thereon of Grant and Santa Fe Counties which were validated, approved and confirmed by Act of Congress, January sixteenth, eighteen hundred and ninety-seven.

Sec. 4. The proper officers of the state shall, as soon as practicable, select and locate the one million acres of land granted to the state by Congress for the payment of the said bonds of Grant and Santa Fe Counties, and sell the same or sufficient thereof to pay the interest and principal of the bonds of Series C issued as provided in section three hereof. The proceeds of rentals and sales of said land shall be kept in a separate fund and applied to the payment of the interest and principal of the bonds of Series C. Whenever there is not sufficient money in said fund to meet the interest and sinking fund requirements therefor, the deficiency shall be paid out of any funds of the state not otherwise appropriated, and shall be repaid to the state or to the several counties which may have furnished any portion thereof under a general levy, out the proceeds subsequently received of rentals and sales of said lands.

Any money received by the state from rentals and sales of said lands in excess of the amounts required for the purposes above-mentioned shall be paid into the current and permanent school funds of the state respectively.

Sec. 5. The legislature shall never enact any law releasing any county, or any of the taxable property therein, from its obligation to pay to the state any moneys expended by the state by reason of its assumption or payment of the debt of such county.

Sec. 6. No law shall ever be passed by the legislature validating or legalizing, directly or indirectly, the militia warrants alleged to be outstanding against the territory of New Mexico, or any portion thereof; and no such warrant shall be prima facie or conclusive evidence of the validity of the debt purporting to be evidenced thereby or by any other militia warrant. This provision shall not be construed as authorizing any suit against the state.

Sec. 7. The state may borrow money not exceeding the sum of two hundred thousand dollars in the aggregate to meet casual deficits or failure in revenue, or for necessary expenses. The state may also contract debts to suppress insurrection and to provide for the public defense.

Sec. 8. No debt other than those specified in the preceding section shall be contracted by or on behalf of this state, unless authorized by law for some specified work or object; which law shall provide for an annual tax levy sufficient to pay the interest and to provide a sinking fund to pay the principal of such debt within fifty years from the time of the contracting thereof. No such law shall take effect until it shall have been submitted to the qualified electors of the state and have received a majority of all the votes cast thereon at a general election; such law shall be published in full in at least one newspaper in each county of the state, if one be published therein, once each week, for four successive weeks next preceding such election. No debt shall be so created if the total indebtedness of the state, exclusive of the debts of the territory, and the several counties thereof, assumed by the state, would thereby be made to exceed one per cent of the assessed valuation of all the property subject to taxation in the state as shown by the preceding general assessment.

Sec. 9. Any money borrowed by the state, or any county, district, or municipality thereof, shall be applied to the purpose for which it was obtained, or to repay such loan, and to no other purpose whatever.

Sec. 10. No county shall borrow money except for the purpose of erecting, remodeling and making additions to necessary public buildings, or constructing or repairing public roads and bridges, and in such cases only after the proposition to create such debt has been submitted to the qualified electors of the county, who paid a property tax therein during the preceding year, and approved by a majority of those voting thereon. No bonds issued for such purpose shall run for more than fifty [50] years. Provided, however, that no moneys derived from general obligation bonds issued and sold hereunder, shall be used for maintaining existing buildings and, if so, such bonds shall be invalid. (As amended November 3, 1964.)

Sec. 11. No school district shall borrow money except for the purpose of erecting, remodeling, making additions to and furnishing school buildings or purchasing or improving school grounds or any combination of these purposes, and in such cases only when the proposition to create the debt has been submitted to a vote of such qualified electors of the district as are owners of real estate within the school district and a majority of those voting on the question have voted in favor of creating such debt. No school district shall ever become indebted in an amount exceeding six per cent [6%] on the assessed valuation of the taxable property within the school district as shown by the preceding general assessment. (As amended September 19, 1933 and September 28, 1965.)

Sec. 12. No city, town or village shall contract any debt except by an ordinance, which shall be irrepealable until the indebtedness therein provided for shall have been fully paid or discharged, and which shall specify the purposes to which the funds to be raised shall be applied, and which shall provide for the levy of a tax, not exceeding twelve [12] mills on the dollar upon all taxable property within such city, town or village, sufficient to pay the interest on, and to extinguish the principal of, such debt within fifty [50] years. The proceeds of such tax shall be applied only to the payment of such interest and principal. No such debt shall be created unless the question of incurring the same shall, at a regular election for councilmen, aldermen or other officers of such city, town or village, or at any special election called for such purpose, have been submitted to a vote of such qualified electors thereof as have paid a property tax therein during the preceding year, and a majority of those voting on the question by ballot deposited in a separate ballot box when voting in a regular election, shall have voted in favor of creating such debt. A proposal which does not receive the required number of votes for adoption at any special election called for that purpose, shall not be resubmitted in any special election within a period of one [1] year. For the purpose, only, of voting on the creation of the debt, any person owning property within the corporate limits of the city, town or village who has paid a property tax therein during the preceding year and who is otherwise qualified to vote in the county where such city, town or village is situated shall be a qualified elector. (As amended November 3, 1964.)

Sec. 13. No county, city, town or village shall ever become indebted to an amount in the aggregate, including existing indebtedness, exceeding four per centum on the value of the taxable property within such county, city, town or village, as shown by the last preceding assessment for state or county taxes; and all bonds or obligations issued in excess of such amount shall be void; provided, that any city, town or village may contract debts in excess of such limitation for the construction or purchase of a system for supplying water, or of a sewer system, for such city, town or village.

Sec. 14. Neither the state, nor any county, school district, or municipality, except as otherwise provided in this Constitution, shall directly or indirectly lend or pledge its credit, or make any donation to or in aid of any person, association or public or private corporation, or in aid of any private enterprise for the construction of any railroad; provided, nothing herein shall be construed to prohibit the state or any county or municipality from making provision for the care and maintenance of sick and indigent persons, nor shall it prohibit the state from establishing a veterans' scholarship program for Vietnam conflict veterans who are post-secondary students at educational institutions under the exclusive control of the state by exempting such veterans from the payment of tuition. For the purposes of this section a "Vietnam conflict veteran" is any person who has been honorably discharged from the armed forces of the United States, who was a resident of New Mexico at the original time of entry into the armed forces from New Mexico and who has been awarded a Vietnam campaign medal for service in the armed forces of this country in Vietnam during the period from August 5, 1964 to the official termination date of the Vietnam conflict as designated by executive order of the president of the United States. The state may also establish by law a program of loans to students of the healing arts, as defined by law, for residents of the state who, in return for the payment of educational expenses, contract with the state to practice their profession for a period of years after graduation within areas of the state designated by law. (As amended November 2, 1971.)

Sec. 15. Nothing in this article shall be construed to prohibit the issue of bonds for the purpose of paying or refunding any valid state, county, district, or municipal bonds and it shall not be necessary to submit the question of the issue of such bonds to a vote as herein provided.

Sec. 16. Laws enacted by the fifth legislature authorizing the issue and sale of state highway bonds for the purpose of providing funds for the construction and improvement of state highways and to enable the state to meet and secure allotments of federal funds to aid in construction and improvement of roads, and laws so enacted authorizing the issue and sale of state highway debentures to anticipate the collection of revenues from motor vehicle licenses and other revenues provided by law for the state road fund, shall take effect without submitting them to the electors of the state, and notwithstanding that the total indebtedness of the state may thereby temporarily exceed one per centum of the assessed valuation of all property subject to taxation in the state. Provided, that the total amount of such state highway bonds payable from proceeds of taxes levied on property outstanding at any one time shall not exceed two million dollars. The legislature shall not enact any law which will decrease the amount of the annual revenues pledged for the payment of state highway debentures or which will divert any of such revenues to any other purpose so long as any of the said debentures issued to anticipate the collection thereof remain unpaid. (As added September 20, 1921.)

ARTICLE X
County and Municipal Corporations

Section 1. The legislature shall at its first session classify the counties and fix salaries for all county officers, which shall also apply to those elected at the first election under this Constitution. And no county officer shall receive to his own use any fees or emoluments other than the annual salary provided by law, and all fees earned by any officer shall be by him collected and paid into the treasury of the county.

Sec. 2. All county officers shall be elected for a term of two years, and after having served two consecutive terms, shall be ineligible to hold any county office for two years thereafter. (As amended November 3, 1914.)

Sec. 3. No county seat, where there are county buildings, shall be removed unless three-fifths of the votes cast by qualified electors on the question of removal at an election called and held as now or hereafter provided by law, be in favor of such removal. The proposition of removal shall not be submitted in the same county oftener than once in eight years.

Sec. 4. (a) The legislature shall, by general law, provide for the formation of combined city and county municipal corporations, and for the manner of determining the territorial limits thereof, each of which shall be known as a "city and county," and, when organized, shall contain a population of at least fifty thousand (50,000) inhabitants. No such city and county shall be formed except by a majority vote of the qualified electors of the area proposed to be included therein, and if the proposed area includes any area not within the existing limits of a city, a majority of those electors living outside the city, voting separately shall be required. Any such city and county shall be permitted to frame a charter for its own government, and amend the same, in the manner provided by the legislature by general law for the formation and organization of such corporations.

(b) Every such charter shall designate the respective officers of such city and county who shall perform the duties imposed by law upon county officers and shall make provisions for the payment of existing city and county indebtedness as hereinafter required. The officers of a city and county, their compensation, qualifications, term of office and manner of election or appointment, shall be as provided for in its charter, subject to general laws and applicable constitutional provisions. The salary of any elective or appointive officer of a city and county shall not be changed after his election or appointment or during his term of office; nor shall the term of any such officer be extended beyond the period for which he is elected or appointed. Every such city and county shall have and enjoy all rights, powers and privileges asserted in its charter not inconsistent with its general laws, and, in addition thereto, such rights, powers, and privileges as may be granted to it, or possessed and enjoyed by cities and counties of like population separately organized.

(c) No city or county government existing outside the territorial limits of such city and county shall exercise any police, taxation or other powers within the territorial limits of such city and county, but all such powers shall be exercised by the city and county and the officers thereof, subject to such constitutional provisions and general laws as apply to either cities or counties.

(d) In case an existing county is divided in the formation of city and county government, such city and county shall be liable for a just proportion of the existing debts or liabilities of the former county and shall account for and pay the county remaining a just proportion of the value of any real estate or other property owned by the former county and taken over by the city and county government, the method of determining such proportion shall be prescribed by general law, but such division shall not affect the rights of creditors.

(e) Nothing herein contained shall be construed to alter or amend the existing constitutional provisions regarding apportionment of representation in the legislature or in the boundaries of legislative districts or judicial districts, nor the jurisdiction or organization of the district or probate courts. (As added September 20, 1949.)

Sec. 5. Any county at the time of the adoption of this amendment, which is less than one hundred forty-four [144] square miles in area and has a population of ten thousand [10,000] or more may become an incorporated county by the following procedure:

A. Upon the filing of a petition containing the signatures of at least ten per cent [10%] of the registered voters in the county, the board of county commissioners shall appoint a charter commission consisting of not less than three [3] persons to draft an incorporated county charter; or

B. The board of county commissioners may, upon its own initiative, appoint a charter commission consisting of not less than three [3] persons to draft an incorporated county charter; and

C. The proposed charter drafted by the charter commission shall be submitted to the qualified voters of the county within one [1] year after the appointment of the commission and if adopted by a majority of the qualified voters voting in the election the county shall become an incorporated county.

The charter of an incorporated county shall provide for the form and organization of the incorporated county government and shall designate those officers which shall be elected, and those officers and employees which shall perform the duties assigned by law to county officers.

An incorporated county may exercise all powers and shall be subject to all limitations granted to municipalities by article 9, section 12 of the Constitution of New Mexico and all powers granted to municipalities by statute.

A charter of an incorporated county shall be amended in accordance with the provisions of the charter.

Nothing herein contained shall be construed to alter or amend the existing constitutional provisions regarding apportionment of representation in the legislature or in the boundaries of legislative districts or judicial districts, nor the jurisdiction or organization of the district or probate courts.

The provisions of this amendment shall be self-executing. (As added November 3, 1964.)

Sec. 6. A. For the purpose of electing some or all of the members of the governing body of a municipality:

(1) the legislature may authorize a municipality by general law to be districted;

(2) if districts have not been established as authorized by law, the governing body of a municipality may, by resolution, authorize the districting of the municipality. The resolution shall not become effective in the municipality until approved by a majority vote in the municipality; and

(3) if districts have not been established as authorized by law or by resolution, the voters of a municipality, by a petition which is signed by not less than five per cent of the registered qualified electors of the municipality and which specifies the number of members of the governing body to be elected from districts, may require the governing body to submit to the registered qualified electors of the municipality, at the next regular municipal election held not less than sixty days after the petition is filed, a resolution requiring the districting of the municipality by its governing body. The resolution shall not become effective in the municipality until approved by a majority vote in the municipality. The signatures for a petition shall be collected within a six-month period.

B. Any member of the governing body of a municipality representing a district shall be a resident of, and elected by, the registered qualified electors of that district.

C. The registered qualified electors of a municipality may adopt, amend or repeal a charter in the manner provided by law. In the absence of law, the governing body of a municipality may appoint a charter commission upon its own initiative or shall appoint a charter commission upon the filing of a petition containing the signatures of at least five per cent of the registered qualified electors of the municipality. The charter commission shall consist of not less than seven members who shall draft a proposed charter. The proposed charter shall be submitted to the registered qualified electors of the municipality within one year from the appointment of the charter commission. If the charter is approved by a majority vote in the municipality, it shall become effective at the time and in the manner provided in the charter.

D. A municipality which adopts a charter may exercise all legislative powers and perform all functions not expressly denied by general law or charter. This grant of powers shall not include the power to enact private or civil laws governing civil relationships except as incident to the exercise of an independent municipal power, nor shall it include the power to provide for a penalty greater than the penalty provided for a petty misdemeanor. No tax imposed by the governing body of a charter municipality, except a tax authorized by general law, shall become effective until approved by a majority vote in the charter municipality.

E. The purpose of this section is to provide for maximum local self-government. A liberal construction shall be given to the powers of municipalities. (Adopted November 3, 1970.)

Sec. 7. In those counties having a population of more than one hundred thousand, as shown by the most recent decennial census, and having a final, full assessed valuation in excess of seventy-five million dollars ($75,000,000), the elected board of county commissioners shall consist of five members. The county shall be divided into five county commission districts which shall be compact, contiguous and as nearly equal in population as practicable. One county commissioner shall reside within, and be elected from, each county commission district. Change of residence to a place outside the district from which a county commissioner was elected shall automatically terminate the service of that commissioner and the office shall be declared vacant.

County commissioners serving on a five-member board of county commissioners shall serve terms of four years, and after having served two consecutive terms, shall be ineligible to hold any county office for four years thereafter.

Provided, that in the first general election immediately following the adoption of this amendment, two county commissioners shall each be elected for a term of two years; two county commissioners shall each be elected for a term of four years; and one county commissioner shall be elected for a term of six years; thereafter, each county commissioner shall be elected for a term of four years. (As added November 6, 1973.)

ARTICLE XI
Corporations Other Than Municipal

Section 1. A permanent commission to consist of three members is hereby created, which shall be known as the "State Corporation Commission."

Sec. 2. The members of the commission shall be elected for the term of six years; provided, that those chosen at the first election for state officers shall immediately qualify and classify themselves by lot, so that one of them shall hold office until two years, one until four years, and one until six years from and after January first, nineteen hundred and thirteen; and thereafter one commissioner shall be elected at each general election.

Sec. 3. No officer, agent or employee of any railway, express, telegraph, telephone, sleeping-car, or other transportation or transmission company, while representing such company, nor any person financially interested therein, shall hold office as a member of the commission, or perform any of the duties thereof, and no commissioner shall be qualified to act upon any matter pending before the commission, in which he is interested, either as principal, agent or attorney.

Sec. 4. The commission shall annually elect one of its members chairman and shall have one clerk, and such other officers, assistants and subordinates as may be prescribed by law, all of whom shall be appointed and subject to removal by the commission. The commission shall prescribe its own rules of order and procedure, except so far as specified in this Constitution. The attorney general of the state, or his legally authorized representative, shall be the attorney for the commission.

Sec. 5. The legislature shall provide suitable quarters for the commission, and funds for its lawful expenses, including necessary traveling expenses, witness fees and mileage, and cost of executing process issued by the commission, or the Supreme Court, or the district courts. The salary of each commissioner shall be prescribed by the legislature. (As amended November 3, 1964.)

Sec. 6. Subject to the provisions of this Constitution, and of such requirements, rules and regulations as may be prescribed by law, the state corporation commission shall be the department of government through which shall be issued all charters for domestic corporations and amendments or extensions thereof, and all licenses to foreign corporations to do business in this state; and through which shall be carried out all the provisions of this Constitution relating to corporations and the laws made in pursuance thereof. The commission shall prescribe the form of all reports which may be required of corporations by this Constitution or by law, and shall collect, receive and preserve such reports, and annually tabulate and publish them. All fees required by law to be paid for the filing of articles of incorporation, reports and other documents, shall be collected by the commission and paid into the state treasury. All charters, papers and documents relating to corporations on file in the office of the secretary of the territory, the commissioner of insurance and all other territorial offices, shall be transferred to the office of the commission.

Sec. 7. The commission shall have power and be charged with the duty of fixing, determining, supervising, regulating and controlling all charges and rates of railway, express, telegraph, telephone, sleeping-car and other transportation and transmission companies and common carriers within the state and of determining any matters of public convenience and necessity relating to such facilities as expressed herein in the manner which has been or shall be provided by law; to require railway companies to provide and maintain adequate depots, stockpens, station buildings, agents and facilities for the accommodation of passengers and for receiving and delivering freight and express; to provide and maintain necessary crossings, culverts and sidings upon and alongside their roadbeds, whenever in the judgment of the commission the public interests demand, and as may be reasonable and just. The commission shall also have power and be charged with the duty to make and enforce reasonable and just rules requiring the supplying of cars and equipment for the use of shippers and passengers, and to require all intrastate railways, transportation companies or common carriers, to provide such reasonable safety appliances in connection with all equipment, as may be necessary and proper for the safety of its employees and the public, and as are now or may be required by the federal laws, rules and regulations governing interstate commerce. The commission shall have power to change or alter such rates, to change, alter or amend its orders, rules, regulations or determinations, and to enforce the same in the manner prescribed herein; Provided, that in the matter of fixing rates of telephone and telegraph companies, due consideration shall be given to the earnings, investment and expenditure as a whole within the state. No general change in a rate, fare or charge shall be collected by any telephone or telegraph company or common carrier until such proposed increase is approved by the commission or, in the event of removal, until such proposed increase is approved by the Supreme Court except as otherwise provided in this Constitution. The commission shall have power to subpoena witnesses and enforce their attendance before the commission, through any district court or the Supreme Court of the state, and through such court to punish for contempt; and it shall have power, upon a hearing, to determine and decide any question given to it herein, and in case of failure or refusal of any person, company or corporation to comply with any order within the time limit therein, unless an order of removal shall have been taken from such order by the company or corporation to the Supreme Court of this state, it shall immediately become the duty of the commission to remove such order, with the evidence adduced upon the hearing, with the documents in the case to the Supreme Court of this state. Any company, corporation or common carrier which does not comply with the order of the commission within the time limited therefor, may file with the commission a petition to remove such cause to the Supreme Court, and in the event of such removal by the company, corporation or common carrier, or other party to such hearing, the Supreme Court may, upon application, in its discretion or of its own motion, require or authorize additional evidence to be taken in such cause; but in the event of removal by the commission, upon failure of the company, corporation or common carrier, no additional evidence shall be allowed. The Supreme Court, for the consideration of such causes arising hereunder, shall be in session at all times, and shall give precedence to such causes. Any party to such hearing before the commission, shall have the same right to remove the order entered therein to the Supreme Court of the state, as given under the provisions hereof to the company or corporation against which such order is directed.

In addition to the other powers vested in the Supreme Court by this Constitution and the laws of the state, the said court shall have the power and it shall be its duty to decide such cases on their merits, and carry into effect its judgments, orders and decrees made in such cases, by fine, forfeiture, mandamus, injunction and contempt or other appropriate proceedings. (As amended November 3, 1964.)

Sec. 8. The commission shall determine no question nor issue any order in relation to the matters specified in the preceding section, until after a public hearing held upon ten [10] days' notice to the parties concerned, except in the case of default after such notice. At any hearing before the commission involving a general change in a rate, fare or charge, the burden of proof to show that the proposed rate, fare or charge is just and reasonable, shall be upon the telephone or telegraph company or common carrier proposing to establish and collect the rate, fare or charge. The commission shall hear and decide applications for a general change in a rate, fare or charge with reasonable promptness. If within six [6] months after having filed such an application the commission has not entered an order disposing of the matter, the company or common carrier may put the proposed change into effect. In the event an aggrieved company or common carrier removes to the Supreme Court a commission order deciding an application for a general change in a rate, fare or charge the Supreme Court may allow the proposed change to be placed into effect under bond in an amount and subject to terms and conditions as it may prescribe. (As amended November 3, 1964.)

Sec. 9. It is hereby made the duty of the commissioners to exercise constant diligence in informing themselves of the rates and charges of transportation and transmission companies and common carriers engaged in the transportation of passengers and property from points in this state to points beyond its limits, and from points in other states to points in this state; and, whenever, it shall come to the knowledge of the commission, by complaint or in any other manner, that the rate charged by any transportation or transmission company or common carrier, on interstate business is unjust, excessive or unreasonable, or that such rates discriminate against the citizens of the state, and in the judgment of the commission such complaint is well founded and the public welfare involved, the commission shall institute and prosecute to a final determination before the interstate commerce commission or commerce court, or any lawful authority having jurisdiction in the premises, such proceedings as it may deem expedient to obtain such relief as conditions may require.

Sec. 10. No transportation or transmission company or common carrier shall charge or receive any greater compensation, in the aggregate, for the transportation as intrastate commerce of passengers, or a like kind of property, or for the transmission of the same kind of message, between points in this state, for a shorter than a longer distance over the same line or route in the same direction, the shorter being included within the longer distance; but this section shall not be construed as authorizing any such company or common carrier to charge or receive as great compensation for a shorter as for a longer distance; provided, that telegraph and telephone companies may, in certain cases, with the approval of the commission, base their charges upon the air-line distances instead of the distances actually traveled by the messages. The commission may from time to time authorize any such company or common carrier to disregard the foregoing provisions of this section, by charging such rates as the commission may prescribe as just and equitable between such company or common carrier and the public, to or from any junction or competitive points, or localities, or where the competition of point located without or within this state may necessitate the prescribing of special rates for the protection of the commerce of this state, or in cases of general epidemics, pestilence, calamitous visitations and other exigencies. This section shall not apply to mileage tickets or to any special excursion or commutation rates; nor to special rates for services rendered in the interest of any public or charitable object, when such tickets or rates shall have been prescribed or authorized by the commission, nor shall it apply to special rates for services rendered to the United States or this state.

Sec. 11. The commission shall have the right at all times to inspect the books, papers and records of all such companies and common carriers doing business in this state, and to require from such companies and common carriers from time to time special reports and statements, under oath, concerning their business. The commissioners shall have the power to administer oaths and to certify to their official acts.

Sec. 12. No corporation in existence at the time of the adoption of this Constitution shall have the benefit of any future legislation, nor shall any amendment or extension to its charter be granted, until such corporation shall have filed in the office of the commission an acceptance of the provisions of this Constitution; provided, however, that whether or not they file such acceptance, such corporations shall be subject to the provisions of this Constitution and the laws of this state.

GENERAL PROVISIONS

Sec. 13. The legislature shall provide for the organization of corporations by general law. All laws relating to corporations may be altered, amended or repealed by the legislature, at any time, when necessary for the public good and general welfare, and all corporations, doing business in this state, may, as to such business, be regulated, limited or restrained by laws not in conflict with the Constitution of the United States or of this Constitution.

Sec. 14. The police power of this state is supreme over all corporations as well as individuals.

Sec. 15. Every railroad, car or express company, shall respectively receive and transport, without delay or discrimination, each other's cars, tonnage or passengers, under such rules and regulations as may be prescribed by the commission.

Sec. 16. All telephone and telegraph lines, operated for hire, shall receive and transmit each other's messages without delay or discrimination, and make and maintain connections with each other's lines, under such rules and regulations as may be prescribed by the commission.

Sec. 17. Any railroad corporation or association organized for the purpose, shall have the right to construct and operate a railroad between any points within this state or elsewhere, and to connect at the state line or elsewhere with the railroads of other states; and, under such terms, order or permission as may be granted in each instance by the commission, shall have the right to cause its road to intersect, connect with or cross any other railroad.

Sec. 18. The right of eminent domain shall never be so abridged or construed as to prevent the legislature from taking the property and franchises of incorporated companies and subjecting them to the public use, the same as the property of individuals.

ARTICLE XII
Education

Section 1. A uniform system of free public schools sufficient for the education of, and open to, all the children of school age in the state shall be established and maintained.

Sec. 2. The permanent school fund of the state shall consist of the proceeds of sales of sections two, sixteen, thirty-two and thirty-six in each township of the state, or the lands selected in lieu thereof; the proceeds of sales of all lands that have been or may hereafter be granted to the state not otherwise appropriated by the terms and conditions of the grant; such portion of the proceeds of sales of land of the United States within the state as has been or may be granted by Congress; also all other grants, gifts and devises made to the state, the purpose of which is not otherwise specified.

Sec. 3. The schools, colleges, universities and other educational institutions provided for by this Constitution shall forever remain under the exclusive control of the state, and no part of the proceeds arising from the sale or disposal of any lands granted to the state by Congress, or any other funds appropriated, levied or collected for educational purposes, shall be used for the support of any sectarian, denominational or private school, college or university.

Sec. 4. All fines and forfeitures collected under general laws; the net proceeds of property that may come to the state by escheat; the rentals of all school lands and other lands granted to the state, the disposition of which is not otherwise provided for by the terms of the grant or by Act of Congress; and the income derived from the permanent school fund, shall constitute the current school fund of the state. (As amended November 2, 1971.)

Sec. 5. Every child of school age and of sufficient physical and mental ability shall be required to attend a public or other school during such period and for such time as may be prescribed by law.

Sec. 6. A. There is hereby created a "state department of public education" and a "state board of education." The state board of education shall determine public school policy and vocational educational policy and shall have control, management and direction of all public schools, pursuant to authority and powers provided by law. The board shall appoint a qualified, experienced educational administrator to be known as the superintendent of public instruction, who shall, subject to the policies established by the board, direct the operation of the state department of public education.

B. The members of the state board of education shall be elected at the general election next following the adoption of this amendment. One member shall be elected from each of the present ten judicial districts. The initial board shall determine by lot from its membership three members to serve terms of two years and three members to serve terms of four years. The remaining of the initial board shall serve terms of six years. Thereafter, as the terms of the initial board members expire, their replacements shall be elected from the same districts for terms of six years.

If additional judicial districts are created the legislature may provide by law for the election by the people of a board of not less than seven members nor more than ten members from board of education districts, created by the legislature.

The governor shall fill vacancies in the board by appointment of a resident from the district in which the vacancy occurs. Appointments shall be made within sixty days after the vacancy occurs. The appointed member shall serve until the next general election, at which time a member shall be elected to complete the original unexpired term.

C. Board members shall be residents of the district they represent. Change of residence of a board member to a place outside the district from which he was elected shall automatically terminate the term of that member. The board members may be removed in the manner in which the legislature may provide by law. (As amended November 4, 1958, effective January 1, 1959.)

Sec. 7. The principal of the permanent school fund, and other permanent funds, shall be invested by a state investment officer in accordance with policy regulations promulgated by a state investment council. The legislature may by a three-fourth's vote of the members elected to each house provide that said funds may be invested in interest-bearing or other securities. All losses from such interest-bearing notes or securities which have definite maturity dates shall be reimbursed by the state.

The state investment officer, in order to realize increased income, may, with the approval of the state investment council, sell interest-bearing notes or securities at less than their original acquisition cost, providing the proceeds are immediately reinvested in sufficiently higher yielding interest-bearing notes or securities, to provide for a portion of the increased interest income to be amortized over the life of the new investment which will restore to the corpus of the fund the amount of the capital loss realized on the sale of the original investment.

In making investments, the state investment officer, under the supervision of the state investment council, shall exercise the judgment and care under the circumstances then prevailing which businessmen of ordinary prudence, discretion and intelligence exercise in the management of their own affairs not in regard to speculation but in regard to the permanent disposition of their funds, considering the probable income as well as the probable safety of their capital; Provided, not more than fifty per cent [50%] of the permanent school fund or other permanent fund, shall be invested at any given time in corporate stocks and bonds nor shall more than ten per cent [10%] of the voting stock of a corporation be held; and Provided further, stocks eligible for purchase shall be restricted to those stocks of businesses incorporated within the United States which have paid dividends for ten [10] consecutive years or longer immediately prior to the date of purchase and which are listed upon a national stock exchange. (As amended November 4, 1958 and September 28, 1965.)

Sec. 8. The legislature shall provide for the training of teachers in the normal schools or otherwise so that they may become proficient in both the English and Spanish languages, to qualify them to teach Spanish-speaking pupils and students in the public schools and educational institutions of the state, and shall provide proper means and methods to facilitate the teaching of the English language and other branches of learning to such pupils and students.

Sec. 9. No religious test shall ever be required as a condition of admission into the public schools or any educational institution of this state, either as a teacher or student, and no teacher or student of such school or institution shall ever be required to attend or participate in any religious service whatsoever.

Sec. 10. Children of Spanish descent in the state of New Mexico shall never be denied the right and privilege of admission and attendance in the public schools or other public educational institutions of the state, and they shall never be classed in separate schools, but shall forever enjoy perfect equality with other children in all public schools and educational institutions of the state, and the legislature shall provide penalties for the violation of this section. This section shall never be amended except upon a vote of the people of this state, in an election at which at least three-fourths of the electors voting in the whole state and at least two-thirds of those voting in each county in the state shall vote for such amendment.

Sec. 11. The University of New Mexico, at Albuquerque; the New Mexico State University, near Las Cruces, formerly known as New Mexico College of Agriculture and Mechanic Arts; the New Mexico Highlands University, at Las Vegas, formerly known as New Mexico Normal University; the Western New Mexico University, at Silver City, formerly known as New Mexico Western College and New Mexico Normal School; the Eastern New Mexico University, at Portales, formerly known as Eastern New Mexico Normal School; the New Mexico Institute of Mining and Technology, at Socorro, formerly known as New Mexico School of Mines; the New Mexico Military Institute, at Roswell, formerly known as New Mexico Military Institute; the New Mexico School for the Visually Handicapped, at Alamogordo, formerly known as New Mexico Institute for the Blind; the New Mexico School for the Deaf, at Santa Fe, formerly known as New Mexico Asylum for the Deaf and Dumb; the Northern New Mexico State School, at El Rito, formerly known as Spanish-American School; are hereby confirmed as state educational institutions. All lands, together with the natural products thereof and the money proceeds of any of the lands and products, held in trust for the institutions, respectively, under their former names, and all properties heretofore granted to, or owned by, or which may hereafter be granted or conveyed to, the institutions respectively, under their former names, shall, in like manner as heretofore, be held in trust for, or owned by or be considered granted to, the institutions individually under their names as herein above adopted and confirmed. The appropriations made and which may hereafter be made to the state by the United States for agriculture and mechanical colleges and experiment stations in connection therewith shall be paid to the New Mexico State University, formerly known as New Mexico College of Agriculture and Mechanic Arts. (As repealed and re-enacted November 8, 1960; as amended November 3, 1964.)

Sec. 12. All lands granted under the provisions of the Act of Congress, entitled, ''An act to enable the people of New Mexico to form a Constitution and state government and be admitted into the union on an equal footing with the original states; and to enable the people of Arizona to form a Constitution and state government and be admitted into the union on an equal footing with the original states,'' for the purposes of said several institutions are hereby accepted and confirmed to said institutions, and shall be exclusively used for the purposes for which they were granted; provided, that one hundred and seventy thousand acres of the land granted by said act for normal school purposes are hereby equally apportioned between said three normal institutions, and the remaining thirty thousand acres thereof is reserved for a normal school which shall be established by the legislature and located in one of the counties of Union, Quay, Curry, Roosevelt, Chaves or Eddy.

Sec. 13. The legislature shall provide for the control and management of each of said institutions by a board of regents for each institution, consisting of five [5] members, who shall be qualified electors of the state of New Mexico, no more than three [3] of whom at the time of their appointment shall be members of the same political party. The governor shall nominate and by and with the consent of the senate shall appoint the members of each board of regents for each of said institutions. The terms of said members shall be for six [6] years, provided that of the five [5] first appointed the terms of two [2] shall be for two [2] years, the terms for two [2] shall be for four [4] years, and the term of one [1] shall be for six years.

Members of the board shall not be removed except for incompetence, neglect of duty or malfeasance in office. Provided, however, no removal shall be made without notice of hearing and an opportunity to be heard having first been given such member. The Supreme Court of the state of New Mexico is hereby given exclusive original jurisdiction over proceedings to remove members of the board under such rules as it may promulgate and its decision in connection with such matters shall be final. (As amended September 20, 1949, effective January 1, 1950.)

Sec. 14. Any elected local school board member is subject to recall by the voters of the school district from which elected. A petition for a recall election must cite grounds of malfeasance or misfeasance in office or violation of the oath of office, by the member concerned. The recall petition shall be signed by registered voters not less in number than thirty-three and one-third percent of those who voted for the office at the last preceding election at which the office was voted upon. The petition shall be filed with the superintendent of schools for the school district who shall determine whether sufficient valid signatures have been submitted and, if so, the superintendent shall call a special election in the school district concerned. If at the special election a majority of the votes cast on the question of recall are in favor thereof, the local school board member is recalled from office and the vacancy shall be filled as provided by law.

This section is self-executing, but legislation may be enacted to facilitate its operation. (As added November 6, 1973.)

ARTICLE XIII
Public Lands

Section 1. All lands belonging to the territory of New Mexico, and all lands granted, transferred or confirmed to the state by Congress, and all lands hereafter acquired, are declared to be public lands of the state to be held or disposed of as may be provided by law for the purposes for which they have been or may be granted, donated or otherwise acquired; provided, that such of school sections two, thirty-two, sixteen and thirty-six as are not contiguous to other state lands shall not be sold within the period of ten years next after the admission of New Mexico as a state for less than ten dollars per acre.

Sec. 2. The commissioner of public lands shall select, locate classify, and have the direction, control, care and disposition of all public lands, under the provisions of the Acts of Congress relating thereto and such regulations as may be provided by law.

Sec. 3. The provisions of the Enabling Act (36 Stat. 557, 563) which prohibit the granting of a patent for a portion of a tract of public lands under sales contract because the full consideration for the entire tract is not or was not paid, are waived with respect to the following sales:

A. Sale of a portion of a tract under sales contract, if the patent to that portion was issued on or before September 4, 1956;

B. Sale of a portion of a tract under sales contract, if the right to purchase the portion is derived from an assignment made on or before September 4, 1956; or

C. Sale of a portion of a tract under sales contract, or under a contract entered into in substitution of such contract, if the right to purchase all other portions of the tract were assigned or relinquished on or before September 4, 1956 by the person holding the contract.

The legislature may enact laws to carry out the purposes of this amendment. (As added November 3, 1964.)

ARTICLE XIV
Public Institutions

Section 1. The penitentiary at Santa Fe, the Miners' Hospital at Raton, the New Mexico State Hospital at Las Vegas, the New Mexico Boys' School at Springer, the Girls' Welfare Home at Albuquerque, the Carrie Tingley Crippled Children's Hospital at Truth or Consequences and the Los Lunas Mental Hospital at Los Lunas are hereby confirmed as state institutions. (As amended September 20, 1955 and November 8, 1960.)

Sec. 2. All lands which have been or which may be granted to the state by Congress for the purpose of said several institutions are hereby accepted for said several institutions with all other grants, donations or devices for the benefit of the same and shall be exclusively used for the purpose for which they were or may be granted, donated or devised.

Sec. 3. Each of said institutions shall be under such control and management as may be provided by law. (As amended September 20, 1955.)

ARTICLE XV
Agriculture and Conservation

Section 1. There shall be a department of agriculture which shall be under the control of the board of regents of the College of Agriculture and Mechanic Arts; and the legislature shall provide lands and funds necessary for experimental farming and demonstrating by said department.

Sec. 2. The police power of the state shall extend to such control of private forest lands as shall be necessary for the prevention and suppression of forest fires.

ARTICLE XVI
Irrigation and Water Rights

Section 1. All existing rights to the use of any waters in this state for any useful or beneficial purpose are hereby recognized and confirmed.

Sec. 2. The unappropriated water of every natural stream, perennial or torrential, within the state of New Mexico, is hereby declared to belong to the public and to be subject to appropriation for beneficial use, in accordance with the laws of the state. Priority of appropriation shall give the better right.

Sec. 3. Beneficial use shall be the basis, the measure and the limit of the right to the use of water.

Sec. 4. The legislature is authorized to provide by law for the organization and operation of drainage districts and systems.

Sec. 5. In any appeal to the district court from the decision, act or refusal to act of any state executive officer or body in matters relating to water rights, the proceeding upon appeal shall be de novo as cases originally docketed in the district court unless otherwise provided by law. (As added November 7, 1967.)

ARTICLE XVII
Mines and Mining

Section 1. There shall be a state mine inspector who shall be appointed by the governor, by and with the advice and consent of the senate, for a term of four years, and whose duties and salary shall be as prescribed by law. The legislature may pass laws prescribing reasonable qualifications for the state mine inspector and deputy mine inspectors, and current legislative enactments prescribing such qualifications are declared to be in full force and effect. (As amended September 19, 1961.)

Sec. 2. The legislature shall enact laws requiring the proper ventilation of mines, the construction and maintenance of escapement shafts or slopes, and the adoption and use of appliances necessary to protect the health and secure the safety of employees therein. No children under the age of fourteen years shall be employed in mines.

ARTICLE XVIII
Militia

Section 1. The militia of this state shall consist of all able-bodied male citizens between the ages of eighteen and forty-five, except such as are exempt by laws of the United States or of this state. The organized militia shall be called the "National Guard of New Mexico," of which the governor shall be the commander in chief.

Sec. 2. The legislature shall provide for the organization, discipline and equipment of the militia, which shall conform as nearly as practicable to the organization, discipline and equipment of the regular army of the United States, and shall provide for the maintenance thereof.

ARTICLE XIX
Amendments

Section 1. Any amendment or amendments to this Constitution may be proposed in either house of the legislature at any regular session thereof; and if a majority of all members elected to each of the two houses voting separately shall vote in favor thereof, such proposed amendment or amendments shall be entered on their respective journals with the yeas and nays thereon.

The secretary of state shall cause any such amendment or amendments to be published in at least one newspaper in every county of the state, where a newspaper is published once each week, for four consecutive weeks, in English and Spanish when newspapers in both of said languages are published in such counties, the last publication to be not more than two weeks prior to the election at which time said amendment or amendments shall be submitted to the electors of the state for their approval or rejection; and the said amendment or amendments shall be voted upon at the next regular election held in said state after the adjournment of the legislature proposing such amendment or amendments, or at such special election to be held not less than six months after the adjournment of said legislature, at such time as said legislature may by law provide. If the same be ratified by a majority of the electors voting thereon such amendment or amendments shall become part of this Constitution. If two or more amendments are proposed, they shall be so submitted as to enable the electors to vote on each of them separately: Provided, That no amendment shall apply to or affect the provisions of sections one and three of article VII hereof, on elective franchise, and sections eight and ten of article XII hereof, on education, unless it be proposed by vote of three-fourths of the members elected to each house and be ratified by a vote of the people of this state in an election at which at least three-fourths of the electors voting in the whole state and at least two-thirds of those voting in each county in the state shall vote for such amendment. (As amended November 7, 1911.)

Sec. 2. Whenever, during the first twenty-five years after the adoption of this Constitution, the legislature, by a three-fourths vote of the members elected to each house, or, after the expiration of said period of twenty-five years, by a two-thirds vote of the members elected to each house, shall deem it necessary to call a convention to revise or amend this Constitution, they shall submit the question of calling such convention to the electors at the next general election, and if a majority of all the electors voting on such question at said election in the state shall vote in favor of calling a convention the legislature shall, at the next session, provide by law for calling the same. Such convention shall consist of at least as many delegates as there are members of the house of representatives. The Constitution adopted by such convention shall have no validity until it has been submitted to and ratified by the people. (As amended November 7, 1911.)

Sec. 3. If this Constitution be in any way so amended as to allow laws to be enacted by direct vote of the electors the laws which may be so enacted shall be only such as might be enacted by the legislature under the provisions of this Constitution. (As amended November 7, 1911.)

Sec. 4. When the United States shall consent thereto, the legislature, by a majority vote of the members in each house, may submit to the people the question of amending any provision of article XXI of this Constitution on compact with the United States to the extent allowed by the Act of Congress permitting the same, and if a majority of the qualified electors who vote upon any such amendment shall vote in favor thereof the said article shall be thereby amended accordingly. (As amended November 7, 1911.)

Sec. 5. The provisions of section one of this article shall not be changed, altered, or abrogated in any manner except through a general convention called to revise this Constitution as herein provided. (As amended November 7, 1911.)

ARTICLE XX
Miscellaneous

Section 1. Every person elected or appointed to any office shall, before entering upon his duties, take and subscribe to an oath or affirmation that he will support the Constitution of the United States and the Constitution and laws of this state, and that he will faithfully and impartially discharge the duties of his office to the best of his ability.

Sec. 2. Every officer, unless removed, shall hold his office until his successor has duly qualified.

Sec. 3. The term of office of every state, county or district officer, except those elected at the first election held under this Constitution, and those elected to fill vacancies, shall commence on the first day of January next after his election.

Sec. 4. If a vacancy occur in the office of district attorney, judge of the

Supreme or district court, or county commissioner, the governor shall fill such vacancy by appointment and such appointee shall hold such office until the next general election. His successor shall be chosen at such election and shall hold his office until the expiration of the original term.

Sec. 5. If, while the senate is not in session, a vacancy occur in any office the incumbent of which was appointed by the governor by and with the advice and consent of the senate, the governor shall appoint some qualified person to fill the same until the next session of the senate; and shall then appoint by and with the advice and consent of the senate some qualified person to fill said office for the period of the unexpired term.

Sec. 6. General elections shall be held in the state on the Tuesday after the first Monday in November in each even-numbered year.

Sec. 7. The returns of all elections for officers who are chosen by the electors of more than one county shall be canvassed by the county canvassing board of each county as to the vote within their respective counties. Said board shall immediately certify the number of votes received by each candidate for such office within such county, to the state canvassing board herein established, which shall canvass and declare the result of the election.

Sec. 8. In the event that New Mexico is admitted into the Union as a state prior to the Tuesday next after the first Monday in November in the year nineteen hundred and twelve, and if no provision has been made by the state legislature therefor, an election shall be held in the state on the said Tuesday next after the first Monday in November, nineteen hundred and twelve, for the election of presidential electors; and such election shall be held as herein provided for the election upon the ratification of this Constitution, and the returns thereof made to, and canvassed and certified by, the state canvassing board as herein provided in case of the election of state officers.

Sec. 9. No officer of the state who receives a salary, shall accept or receive to his own use any compensation, fees, allowance, or emoluments for or on account of his office, in any form whatever, except the salary provided by law.

Sec. 10. The legislature shall enact suitable laws for the regulation of the employment of children.

Sec. 11. Women may hold the office of notary public and such other appointive offices as may be provided by law.

Sec. 12. For the first twenty years after this Constitution goes into effect all laws passed by the legislature shall be published in both the English and Spanish languages and thereafter such publication shall be made as the legislature may provide.

Sec. 13. The use of wines solely for sacramental purposes under church authority at any place within the state shall never be prohibited.

Sec. 14. It shall not be lawful for the governor, any member of the state board of equalization, any member of the corporation commission, any judge of the Supreme or district court, any district attorney, any county commissioner or any county assessor, during his term of office to accept, hold or use any free pass; or purchase, receive or accept transportation over any railroad within this state for himself or his family upon terms not open to the general public; and any person violating the provisions hereof shall, upon conviction in a court of a competent jurisdiction, be punished as provided in sections thirty-seven and forty of the article on legislative department in this Constitution.

Sec. 15. The penitentiary is a reformatory and an industrial school, and all persons confined therein shall, so far as consistent with discipline and the public interest, be employed in some beneficial industry; and where a convict has a dependent family, his net earnings shall be paid to said family if necessary for their support.

Sec. 16. Every person, receiver or corporation owning or operating a railroad within this state shall be liable in damages for injury to, or the death of, any person in its employ, resulting from the negligence, in whole or in part, of said owner or operator, or of any of the officers, agents or employees thereof, or by reason of any defect or insufficiency, due to its negligence, in whole or in part, in its cars, engines, appliances, machinery, track, roadbed works or other equipment.

An action for negligently causing the death of an employee as above provided shall be maintained by the executor or administrator for the benefit of the employee's surviving widow or husband and children; or if none, then his parents; or if none, then the next of kin dependent upon said deceased. The amount recovered may be distributed as provided by law. Any contract or agreement made in advance of such injury with any employee waiving or limiting any right to recover such damages shall be void.

This provision shall not be construed to affect the provisions of section two of article twenty-two of this Constitution, being the article upon Schedule.

Sec. 17. [**On public school textbooks; repealed 1971.**]

Sec. 18. The leasing of convict labor by the state is hereby prohibited.

Sec. 19. Eight hours shall constitute a day's work in all cases of employment by and on behalf of the state or any county or municipality thereof.

Sec. 20. Any person held by a committing magistrate to await the action of the grand jury on a charge of felony or other infamous crime, may in open court with the consent of the court and the district attorney, to be entered upon the record, waive indictment and plead to an information in the form of an indictment filed by the district attorney, and further proceedings shall then be had upon said information with like force and effect as though it were an indictment duly returned by the grand jury.

Sec. 21. The protection of the state's beautiful and healthful environment is hereby declared to be of fundamental importance to the public interest, health, safety and general welfare. The legislature shall provide for control of pollution and control of despoilment of the air, water and other natural resources of this state, consistent with the use and development of these resources for the maximum benefit of the people. (As added November 2, 1971.)

ARTICLE XXI
Compact with the United States
PREAMBLE

In compliance with the requirements of the Act of Congress, entitled, "An act to enable the people of New Mexico to form a Constitution and state government and be admitted into the Union on an equal footing with the original states; and to enable the people of Arizona to form a Constitution and state government and be admitted into the Union on an equal footing with the original states," approved June twentieth, nineteen hundred and ten, it is hereby provided:

Section 1. Perfect toleration of religious sentiment shall be secured, and no inhabitant of this state shall ever be molested in person or property on account of his or her mode of religious worship. Polygamous or plural marriages and polygamous cohabitation are forever prohibited. (As amended September 15, 1953.)

Sec. 2. The people inhabiting this state do agree and declare that they forever disclaim all right and title to the unappropriated and ungranted public lands lying within the boundaries thereof, and to all lands lying within said boundaries owned or held by any Indian or Indian tribes, the right or title to which shall have been acquired through the United States, or any prior sovereignty; and that until the title of such Indian or Indian tribes shall have been extinguished the same shall be and remain subject to the disposition and under the absolute jurisdiction and control of the Congress of the United States; and that the lands and other property belonging to citizens of the United States residing without this state shall never be taxed at a higher rate than the lands and other property belonging to residents thereof; that no taxes shall be imposed by this state upon lands or property therein belonging to or which may hereafter be acquired by the United States or reserved for its use; but nothing herein shall preclude this state from taxing as other lands and property are taxed, any lands and other property outside of an Indian reservation, owned or held by any Indian, save and except such lands as have been granted or acquired as aforesaid, or as may be granted or confirmed to any Indian or Indians under any Act of Congress; but all such lands shall be exempt from taxation by this state so long and to such extent as the Congress of the United States has prescribed or may hereafter prescribe.

Sec. 3. The debts and liabilities of the territory of New Mexico and the debts of the counties thereof, which were valid and subsisting on the twentieth day of June, nineteen hundred and ten, are hereby assumed and shall be paid by this state; and this state shall, as to all such debts and liabilities, be subrogated to all the rights, including rights of indemnity and reimbursement, existing in favor of said territory or of any of the several counties thereof on said date. Nothing in this article shall be construed as validating or in any manner legalizing any territorial, county, municipal or other bonds, warrants, obligations, or evidences of indebtedness of, or claims against, said territory or any of the counties or municipalities thereof which now are or may be, at the time this state is admitted, invalid and illegal; nor shall the legislature of this state pass any law in any manner validating or legalizing the same.

Sec. 4. Provision shall be made for the establishment and maintenance of a system of public schools which shall be open to all the children of the state and free from sectarian control, and said schools shall always be conducted in English.

Sec. 5. This state shall never enact any law restricting or abridging the right of suffrage on account of race, color or previous condition of servitude. (As amended November 5, 1912.)

Sec. 6. The capital of this state shall, until changed by the electors voting at an election provided for by the legislature of this state for that purpose, be at the city of Santa Fe, but no such election shall be called or provided for prior to the thirty-first day of December, nineteen hundred and twenty-five.

Sec. 7. There are hereby reserved to the United States, with full acquiescence of the people of this state, all rights and powers for the carrying out of the provisions by the United States of the Act of Congress, entitled, "An act appropriating the receipts from the sale and disposal of public lands in certain states and territories to the construction of irrigation works for the reclamation of arid lands," approved June seventeenth, nineteen hundred and two, and acts amendatory thereof or supplementary thereto, to the same extent as if this state had remained a territory.

Sec. 8. Whenever hereafter any of the lands contained within Indian reservations or allotments in this state shall be allotted, sold, reserved or otherwise disposed of, they shall be subject for a period of twenty-five years after such allotment, sale, reservation or other disposal, to all the laws of the United States prohibiting the introduction of liquor into the Indian country; and the terms ''Indian'' and ''Indian country'' shall include the Pueblo Indians of New Mexico and the lands owned or occupied by them on the twentieth day of June, nineteen hundred and ten, or which are occupied by them at the time of the admission of New Mexico as a state.

Sec. 9. This state and its people consent to all and singular the provisions of the said Act of Congress, approved June twentieth, nineteen hundred and ten, concerning the lands by said act granted or confirmed to this state, the terms and conditions upon which said grants and confirmations were made and the means and manner of enforcing such terms and conditions, all in every respect and particular as in said act provided.

Sec. 10. This ordinance is irrevocable without the consent of the United States and the people of this state, and no change or abrogation of this ordinance, in whole or in part, shall be made by any constitutional amendment without the consent of Congress.

Sec. 11. This state and its people consent to the provisions of the Act of Congress, approved June 15, 1926, providing for such exchanges and the governor and other state officers mentioned in said act are hereby authorized to execute the necessary instrument or instruments to effect the exchange of lands therein provided for with the government of the United States; Provided that in the determination of values of the lands now owned by the state of New Mexico, the value of the lands, the timber thereon and mineral rights pertaining thereto shall control the determination of value. The legislature may enact laws for the carrying out of the provisions hereof in accordance herewith. (As added November 8, 1932.)

ARTICLE XXII
Schedule

That no inconvenience may arise by reason of the change from a territorial to a state form of government, it is declared and ordained:

Section 1. This Constitution shall take effect and be in full force immediately upon the admission of New Mexico into the Union as a state.

Sec. 2. Until otherwise provided by law, the Act of Congress of the United States, entitled, ''An act relating to liability of common carriers, by railroads to their employees in certain cases,'' approved April twenty-two, nineteen hundred and eight, and all acts amendatory thereof, shall be and remain in force in this state to the same extent that they have been in force in the territory of New Mexico.

Sec. 3. Until otherwise provided by law, the Act of Congress, entitled, ''An act for the protection of the lives of miners,'' approved March three, eighteen hundred and ninety-one, and all acts amendatory thereof, shall be and remain in force in this state to the same extent that they have been in force in the territory of New Mexico; the words ''Governor of the State,'' are hereby substituted for the words ''Governor of such organized territory,'' and for the words ''Secretary of the Interior'' wherever the same appear in said acts; and the chief mine inspector for the territory of New Mexico, appointed by the President of the United States, is hereby authorized to perform the duties prescribed by said acts until superseded by the ''inspector of mines'' appointed by the governor, as elsewhere provided by the Constitution, and he shall receive the same compensation from the state, as he received from the United States.

Sec. 4. All laws of the territory of New Mexico in force at the time of its admission into the Union as a state, not inconsistent with this Constitution, shall be and remain in force as the laws of the state until they expire by their own limitation, or are altered or repealed; and all rights, actions, claims, contracts, liabilities and obligations, shall continue and remain unaffected by the change in the form of government.

Sec. 5. The pardoning power herein granted shall extend to all persons who have been convicted of offenses against the laws of the territory of New Mexico.

Sec. 6. All property, real and personal, and all moneys, credits, claims and choses in action belonging to the territory of New Mexico, shall become the property of this state; and all debts, taxes, fines, penalties, escheats and forfeitures, which have accrued or may accrue to said territory, shall inure to this state.

Sec. 7. All recognizances, bonds, obligations and undertakings entered into or executed to the territory of New Mexico, or to any county, school district, municipality, officer or official board therein, shall remain valid according to the terms thereof, and may be sued upon and recovered by the proper authority under the state law.

Sec. 8. All lawful process, writs, judgments, decrees, convictions, and sentences issued, rendered, had or pronounced, in force at the time of the admission of the state, shall continue and remain in force to the same extent as if the change of government had not occurred, and shall be enforced and executed under the laws of the state.

Sec. 9. All courts existing, and all persons holding offices or appointments under the authority of said territory, at the time of the admission of the state, shall continue to hold and exercise their respective jurisdictions, functions, offices and appointments until superseded by the courts, officers, or authorities provided for by this Constitution.

Until otherwise provided by law, the seal of the territory shall be used as the seal of the state, and the seals of the several courts, officers and official boards in the territory shall be used as the seals of the corresponding courts, officers and official boards in the state; and for any new court, office or board created by this Constitution, a seal may be adopted by the judge of said court, or the incumbent of said office, or by the said board.

Sec. 10. All suits, indictments, criminal actions, bonds, process, matters and proceedings pending in any of the courts in the territory of New Mexico at the time of the organization of the courts provided for in this Constitution shall be transferred to and proceed to determination in such courts of like or corresponding jurisdiction. And all civil causes of action and criminal offenses which shall have been commenced, or indictment found, shall be subject to action, prosecution, indictment and review in the proper courts of the state, in like manner and to the same extent as if the state had been created and said courts established prior to the accrual of such causes of action and the commission of such offenses.

Sec. 11. This Constitution shall be signed by the president and secretary of the constitutional convention, and such delegates as desire to sign the same, and shall be deposited in the office of the secretary of the territory where it may be signed at any time by any delegate.

Sec. 12. All lawful debts and obligations of the several counties of the territory of New Mexico not assumed by the state and of the school districts, municipalities, irrigation districts and improvement districts, therein, existing at the time of its admission as a state, shall remain valid and unaffected by the change of government, until paid or refunded according to law; and all counties, municipalities and districts in said territory shall continue with the same names, boundaries and rights until changed in accordance with the Constitution and laws of the state.

Sec. 13. This Constitution shall be submitted to the people of New Mexico for ratification at an election to be held on the twenty-first day of January, nineteen hundred and eleven, at which election the qualified voters of New Mexico shall vote directly for or against the same, and the governor of the territory of New Mexico shall forthwith issue his proclamation ordering said election to be held on said day.

Except as to the manner of making returns of said election and canvassing and certifying the result thereof, said election shall be held and conducted in the manner prescribed by the laws of New Mexico now in force.

Sec. 14. The ballots cast at said election in favor of the ratification of this Constitution shall have printed or written thereon in both English and Spanish the words "For the Constitution"; and those against the ratification of the Constitution shall have written or printed thereon in both English and Spanish the words "Against the Constitution"; and shall be counted and returned accordingly.

Sec. 15. The returns of said election shall be made by the election officers direct to the secretary of the territory of New Mexico at Santa Fe, who, with the governor and the chief justice of said territory, shall constitute a canvassing board, and they, or any two of them, shall meet at said city of Santa Fe on the third Monday after said election and shall canvass the same. Said canvassing board shall make and file with the secretary of the territory of New Mexico, a certificate signed by at least two of them, setting forth the number of votes cast at said election for or against the Constitution, respectively.

Sec. 16. If a majority of the legal votes cast at said election as certified to by said canvassing board, shall be for Constitution, it shall be deemed to be duly ratified by the people of New Mexico and the secretary of the territory of New Mexico shall forthwith cause to be submitted to the President of the United States and to Congress for approval, a certified copy of this Constitution, together with the statement of the votes cast thereon.

Sec. 17. If Congress and the President approve this Constitution, or if the President approves the same and Congress fails to disapprove the same during the next regular session thereof, the governor of New Mexico shall, within thirty days after receipt of notification from the President certifying said facts, issue his proclamation for an election at which officers for a full state government, including a governor, county officers, members of the state legislature, two representatives in Congress to be elected at large from the state, and such other officers as this Constitution prescribes, shall be chosen by the people; said election to take place not earlier than sixty days nor later than ninety days after the date of said proclamation by the governor ordering the same.

Sec. 18. Said last-mentioned election shall be held, the returns thereof made, canvassed and certified to by the secretary of said territory, in the same manner, and under the same laws, including those as to qualifications of electors, shall be applicable thereto, as hereinbefore prescribed for holding, making of the returns, canvassing and certifying the same, of the election for the ratification or rejection of this Constitution.

When said election of state and county officers, members of the legislature, representatives in Congress, and other officers provided for in this

Constitution, shall be held and the returns thereof made, canvassed and certified as hereinbefore provided, the governor of the territory of New Mexico shall immediately certify the result of said election, as canvassed and certified as hereinbefore provided, to the President of the United States.

Sec. 19. Within thirty days after the issuance by the President of the United States of his proclamation announcing the result of said election so ascertained, all officers elected at such election, except members of the legislature, shall take the oath of office and give bond as required by this Constitution or by the laws of the territory of New Mexico in case of like officers in the territory, county or district, and shall thereupon enter upon the duties of their respective offices; but the legislature may by law require such officers to give other or additional bonds as a condition of their continuance in office.

Sec. 20. The governor of the state, immediately upon his qualifying and entering upon the duties of his office, shall issue his proclamation convening the legislature at the seat of government on a day to be specified therein, not less than thirty nor more than sixty days after the date of said proclamation.

The members-elect of the legislature shall meet on the day specified, take the oath required by this Constitution and within ten days after organization shall proceed to the election of two senators of the United States for the state of New Mexico, in the manner prescribed by the Constitution and laws of the United States; and the governor and secretary of the state of New Mexico shall certify the election of the senators and representatives in Congress in the manner required by law.

Sec. 21. The legislature shall pass all necessary laws to carry into effect the provisions of this Constitution.

Sec. 22. The term of office of all officers elected at the election aforesaid shall commence on the date of their qualification and shall expire at the same time as if they had been elected on the Tuesday next after the first Monday of November in the year nineteen hundred and twelve.

ARTICLE XXIII
Intoxicating Liquors [Repealed 1933.]

ARTICLE XXIV
Leases on State Land

Section 1. Leases and other contracts, reserving a royalty to the state, for the development and production of any and all minerals or for the development and operation of geothermal steam and waters on lands granted or confirmed to the state of New Mexico by the Act of Congress of June 20, 1910, entitled "An act to enable the people of New Mexico to form a Constitution and state government and be admitted into the union on an equal footing with the original states," may be made under such provisions relating to the necessity or requirement for or the mode and manner of appraisement, advertisement and competitive bidding, and containing such terms and provisions, as may be provided by act of the legislature; the rentals, royalties and other proceeds therefrom to be applied and conserved in accordance with the provisions of said act of congress for the support or in aid of the common schools, or for the attainment of the respective purposes for which the several grants were made. (As added November 6, 1928; as amended November 7, 1967.)

SIGNERS OF THE CONSTITUTION AS ORIGINALLY ADOPTED

CHARLES A. SPIESS,
PRESIDENT OF THE CONSTITUTIONAL
CONVENTION.

GEO. W. ARMIJO, SECRETARY.
I. ARMIJO
W.E. GARRISON
FLOYD C. FIELD
RAYMUNDO HARRISON
JOHN G. CLANCEY
E.A. MIERA
J.M. CUNNINGHAM
REED HOLLOMAN
T.D. BURNS
E.G. STOVER
MALAQUIAS MARTINEZ
ANTONIO A. SEDILLO
JUAN NAVARRO
GEORGE W. BAKER
FRED S. BROWN
W.E. LINDSEY
DANIEL CASSIDY
GREGORY PAGE
FRANK W. PARKER
NESTOR MONTOYA
CHAS. H. KOHN
VENCESLAO JARAMILLO
M.L. STERN
CANDELARIO VIGIL
FRANCIS E. WOOD
HARRY W. KELLY
EUFRACIO F. GALLEGOS
SOLOMON LUNA
ANICETO ABEYTIA
H.O. BURSUM
STEPHEN B. DAVIS, JR.
SQUIRE HARTT, JR.
BENJ. F. PANKEY
NORMAN W. BARTLETT
THOMAS H. O'BRIEN
ONESIMO G. MARTINEZ
GEORGE S. BROWN
JOSE D. SENA
MARGARITO ROMERO
VICTOR ORTEGA
N. SEGURA
T.B. CATRON
HERBERT F. RAYNOLDS
CHARLES SPRINGER
RUBEN WOODFORD HEFLIN
M.D. TAYLOR

ANDREW H. HUDSPETH
CHARLES CLAYBORNE DAVIDSON
M.P. SKEEN
EDWARD D. TITTMANN
THOS. JEWETT MABRY
JAMES A. HALL
JOHN H. CANNING
ACASIO GALLEGOS
ATANACIO ROIBAL
CHAS. E. MILLER
JOSE AMADO LUCERO
WILLIAM MCKEAN
PERFECTO ESQUIBEL
ANASTACIO MEDINA
CLARENCE J. ROBERTS
JACOBO J. ARAGON
GEORGE W. PRICHARD
WM. MCINTOSH
A.B. MCDONALD
ANASTACIO GUTIERREZ
J.B. GILCHRIST
G.E. MOFFETT
GRANVILLE A. RICHARDSON
JNO. J. HINKLE
C.M. COMPTON
FRANK H. WINSTON
W.D. MURRAY
SILVESTRE MIRABAL
SALOME MARTINEZ
H.M. DOUGHERTY
C.R. BRICE
LUCIANO MAES
SAMUEL ELDODT
FRANCISCO GUANA
E.M. LUCERO
ARTHUR H. HARLLEE
ALBERT B. FALL
EUGENIO ROMERO
ALEJANDRO SANDOVAL
J. FRANK ROMERO
TRANQUILINO LABADIE
WILLIAM B. WALTON
J.W. CHILDERS
JOHN BECKER
JOHN LEE HOUSE
ED. F. SAXON
J.L. LAWSON